On the Fence

On the Fence

A Parent's Handbook of Horseback Riding

JANET BARRETT

Howell
Book House™

Copyright © 2006 by Wiley Publishing, Inc., Hoboken, New Jersey. All rights reserved.

Howell Book House
Published by Wiley Publishing, Inc., Hoboken, New Jersey

For general information on our other products and services or to obtain technical support please contact our Customer Care Department within the U.S. at (800) 762-2974, outside the U.S. at (317) 572-3993 or fax (317) 572-4002.

Wiley also publishes its books in a variety of electronic formats. Some content that appears in print may not be available in electronic books. For more information about Wiley products, please visit our web site at www.wiley.com.

Library of Congress Cataloging-in-Publication Data:
Barrett, Janet, date.
 On the fence : a parent's handbook of horseback riding / Janet Barrett.
   p. cm.
 ISBN-13: 978-0-471-75474-9 (pbk. : alk. paper)
 ISBN-10: 0-471-75474-9 (pbk. : alk. paper)
 1. Horsemanship. I. Title.

SF309.B323 2006
798.2—dc22

                                        2005027094

Printed in the United States of America

10 9 8 7 6 5 4 3 2 1

Book design by Scott Meola, with Melissa Auciello-Brogan and Elizabeth Brooks
Cover design by José Almaguer
Book production by Wiley Publishing, Inc. Composition Services

Contents

Contents

Contents

To my husband, Walter Terlecki, and to the memory of Rio

Acknowledgments

To some wonderful friends for their support: Angele McGrady, for her unending encouragement; Cynthia Parkinson, for reading the manuscript through the eyes of the uninitiated and offering many excellent suggestions; and Dawn Papachristopoulos, her late husband, Theodor, and daughter, Amy, for being my special role models.

To Kitty Stalsburg, program director of High Hopes Therapeutic Riding, Inc., in Old Lyme, Connecticut, for helping me to appreciate how much is available to children with special challenges.

To Roxane Cerda, senior editor, for her enthusiasm and support; and to Kitty Jarrett, development editor, for all her help with this project.

And to the many parents I've met through my years in the sport—people standing at the fence, as happy to talk as I was, who shared many of their delights and concerns as they watched their children learning how to ride.

Chapter One

So, Your Child Wants to Ride a Horse

*I*t started out with such a familiar ring, you only half paid attention.

"Hey, mom, you know what I want to do?"

"No. What?"

"I want to ride a horse."

Pause. Long pause. You'd heard that question a thousand times before, but this answer caught you completely by surprise.

And there was such intensity. "Can I, *please? Can I?*"

A jumble of thoughts raced through your mind, if not right out of your mouth. "You want to do *what?* Whatever gave you that idea?" Or maybe, "I don't know, ask your father." Or an incredulous, "Ride a *horse?*" No, it wasn't what you expected. But if you have opened the cover of this book, maybe you are willing to give it some thought.

Of course, there are many variations on this opening scenario. In fact, parents, noticing a child's interest in horses, will often be the first to think about riding lessons. But there the idea sits, for lack of knowing how to proceed.

Now this book can guide you by answering your questions, helping you avoid the pitfalls, and trying to ensure that you and

1

your child will have a positive, enjoyable experience in the world of horseback riding.

The idea for this book came out of my own experience, though I was neither a child rider nor the parent of one. I actually took up riding seriously as an adult, starting as a beginning rider at thirty-eight, to be exact. Because of my age, however, I got to know lots of parents. And, as I progressed, I helped to answer many of their questions.

As you read on, you will notice that I refer to the young rider as "she" and the instructor as "he." To be sure, there are many young boys beginning to ride and women instructing them, and my choice is obviously not politically correct. It is merely meant to simplify the use of pronouns. You can switch them in your mind's eye to suit your own situation.

Have you noticed how many children are intrigued by horses from a very early age? Whether they are the polished mounted police horses used in cities, those graceful horses ambling about as they grazed in rural pastures, or the spirited horses seen in Hollywood Westerns, they captivate children. Yet, unless you, another family member, or a close friend was or is involved in the sport, from a distance, riding can seem rather intimidating and inaccessible, not to mention costly. It doesn't have to be any of those things.

How you react to your child's insistence on riding a horse probably has a lot to do with your own experience or lack thereof. If you rode horses when you were a youngster and remember it as being fun and exciting, chances are you will be receptive to your child's wish to do the same. All too often, it is the other memories that surface, however, such as remembering yourself in an unsafe riding situation and how you became frightened or, worse yet, hurt because of it. Now, faced with the prospect of your child riding a horse, all your old fears and negative responses come flooding back. Then again, you may never have ridden a horse or perhaps even been near one. And you are still shaking your head, trying to figure out how your child ever came up with this idea in the first place.

Try to look at horseback riding as you would any other sport your child wishes to pursue. She needs proper education to ensure her enjoyment and safety. As with many other sports— among them bicycling, swimming, skiing, ice skating, tennis, football, and in-line skating—the risks of injury are high and the pleasure is minimal *unless you learn how to do them properly.*

Given the proper exposure and training, horseback riding can provide your child with a focus, an involvement, a love, and a skill that will bring her many happy hours and may even last a lifetime. And riding, contrary to what you might think if you have a child who has a physical or mental disability, may be an activity that she, too, can participate in. The appendix provides an in-depth look at therapeutic riding, how to find and evaluate a program or center, and the potential benefits for those who participate.

Whether your child is taught English hunt seat or Western stock seat, learns dressage, goes on to ride hunters or jumpers, barrel races, gets involved in eventing (also known as combined training), or finds that the thing she enjoys most is having a good time trail riding, the beginning is essentially the same. You, as a parent, need to find the best possible situation for the both of you, so that your child can begin to experience the fun that is so much a part of horseback riding.

One Sport, Many Choices

Horseback riders tend to fall into one of two major categories: They are mainly "English" (English hunt seat) riders or "Western" (Western stock seat) riders. While the type of horse they all ride is the same animal, the favored breeds are different, as is the training for both horse and rider.

Riders usually become proficient in one discipline or another, a choice that depends largely on where they live and what their friends do and, certainly, what appeals to them. Horses, too, are broke to one style or another, and unless they switch disciplines with some regularity, it will take some retraining for them to do so.

If people stay in the sport long enough, many of them eventually try a little bit of everything. Even if you are a dedicated English rider, it's fun to sit in a Western saddle and see how well you do riding Western. And what an eye-opener it is for the inexperienced to sit on a reining horse, for instance, and feel firsthand the subtle yet high degree of training involved there!

My own background, just as is true for many others, is the product of an early choice. Living in the northeast United States, I began and continued to ride English hunt seat, coupled with many years of dressage. But, as I found out myself, trying whatever else comes along only adds to your know-how, and I encourage other riders to do it. This is a huge and diverse sport and, I promise, you will never tire of watching and learning about other riders' disciplines. As you read this book, I'm sure my "English" point of view will come through, but hopefully so will my enthusiasm for anyone coming into the sport, wherever he or she chooses to be.

While English and Western are the two main styles of riding—riding "camps," if you like—they are just the tip of the iceberg of the myriad disciplines for horse and rider. Nevertheless, in all parts of the sport, common elements and how you, as a parent, will interpret them are a constant. Wherever you live, how you judge happy, healthy horses and well-run stables is the same, as is evaluating instructors and lessons. This is also true about deciding whether your child should go to horse shows and, overall, the importance of your input as you proceed.

Whether your child wears a hunt cap or a cowboy hat, learns to trot or jog, lope or canter, show over fences or traverse bridges and go through gates will not affect your ability to help her enjoy the world of horseback riding.

Introducing the Horse

The biggest dog in your neighborhood, that strapping Great Dane or lumbering Newfoundland all the kids play with, will be dwarfed by a horse.

A horse's size alone can be rather startling. The animal that your child proposes to ride generally ranges from a 500- to 600-pound pony to a 1,000-pound horse. That's the average. There are even smaller ponies for the littlest riders, and much larger horses, though it's unlikely that a child would learn to ride the likes of a Belgian Draft or a Clydesdale. Stand next to one of these sometime, and you will see what *big* is!

Now that the United States is a thoroughly mechanized nation, horses in the United States are, with few exceptions, used for recreational pursuits. Beautiful, graceful, athletic creatures, they can perform a variety of feats for our enjoyment. They are racehorses, ridden by jockeys around flat tracks and over hedges and other natural hurdles in steeplechase races; they pull their drivers in sulkies in trotting and pacing races; they are pleasure horses, generally ridden outdoors on trails or in other open areas; and they are field hunters or foxhunters, who go cross-country over fences in search of the elusive fox or his scent. They are show horses, who compete in a myriad of disciplines, among them as hunters and jumpers, in dressage, saddle seat, and three-day eventing. They are Western stock, trail, and competition horses; they compete in endurance races and rodeos; and they play polo. Some of them also earn a living as police horses, carriage and parade horses, cattle herders, and in theatrical ventures from television commercials to feature films. And they comprise one last and very special group, remembered fondly by name and deed years after they have completed their job: the school horses who teach our children how to ride.

Though nonhorse people might debate horses' intelligence— and, in truth, on an intelligence scale, other animals surpass them—once you have spent any amount of time with horses, you will likely be persuaded otherwise. They are sensitive and intuitive, each with a definite personality. Not uncommonly, the same horse will take care of a beginning rider with patience and forgiveness, yet make a fool out of an experienced rider who gets "too big for her britches, trying to show a horse what's what."

Remember, though, that while most horses respond to care and kindness and need not be feared, next to a child even the smallest pony is a powerful animal who must be respected at all times. Keeping that in mind, part of the pleasure of riding is the love and close association that is possible between horse and rider. For the child beginning to ride, this special friendship is a wonderful part of the whole experience.

First of All, Riding Is Fun

Ask most youngsters why they ride and, chances are, the number one response will be "because it's fun." They may also add that it is exciting, even thrilling, although such words are often just mirrored in a child's happy face and sparkling eyes.

One thing is for sure: If your child likes the first experience well enough to come back—and if it is your child's wish, not just yours—chances are very good that she will find riding fun. Frankly, if it is not fun, a parent will have little or no success in getting a child to stick with the sport anyway. Or if the child does, it won't be a very happy experience.

Forcing a child to go on when she seems less than enthusiastic after a lesson or two can be detrimental. All the defense mechanisms go up—the child is unwilling, lacks attention, is easily embarrassed, and is even downright scared—all of which can turn something that should and could be enjoyable into an unpleasant, unproductive, and even dangerous episode. When given a choice, a child who decides she doesn't want to ride now may decide to try again at some later time.

And let's face it, other than the parent's disappointment if a child does not continue a family tradition of riding or some other reason along those lines, riding is far from critical to her well-being. A youngster will survive, no doubt very happily, without ever getting on a horse.

However, learning to ride and being around horses can most certainly enrich a child's early years and, if she continues riding, the rest of her life. Beyond fun, it can impart a series of solid and long-lasting benefits. The sense of accomplishment, plus the companionship with horses and friendship with other riders, will long be remembered.

Benefits of Riding

At a time when health authorities are bemoaning the overweight, "couch potato" existence of many of our nation's children, riding is a good, physical, outdoor-indoor activity that can help to promote fitness. As a matter of fact, jockeys are considered the second fittest athletes, right behind marathon runners. Like learning to swim, ride a bicycle, or play tennis, riding takes hard work, and it also requires concentration, comprehension, and the development of skill to do it properly. When done properly, it is exhilarating, never drudgery.

Aside from swimming, which experts agree is the best all-around exercise there is, riding can give more to a person, in a myriad of ways, than any other activity available.

George Steinbrenner, the New York Yankees owner and a familiar face in horse racing circles, was quoted years ago as saying, "With all the things going on in the world, there is nothing better for a kid than to be raised around horses. Show me a kid who's been raised around horses and I'll show you a kid that turns out to be a fine person in almost every case" (Editorial, *Eastern Horse World*, March 1, 1987).

Horse people everywhere will second Steinbrenner's sentiment wholeheartedly, and many will tell you story after story of youngsters who survived negative influences and stayed on track because (and in some cases *only* because) of their involvement with horses. Others, with physical and mental challenges, have also benefited greatly. Obviously, if your youngster catches you off guard by popping the question, you know she is ready to ride. But even if it is your idea, try to finesse it so that it winds up being your child who says, "I want to do it." With that commitment, in all probability, she will succeed.

Children who take to riding are seldom lukewarm about it. Quite the opposite: They are quickly enamored with the sport and its surroundings and look forward to coming to the stable as often as they can, even daily if they can persuade their parents. The involvement provides a productive channel for energies, both mental and physical, that can, quite bluntly, help keep youngsters off the streets and away from drugs, alcohol, and other destructive pursuits.

Riding teaches responsibility, patience, coordination, concentration, fitness, application, accomplishment, achievement, sportsmanship, humility, lifelong skills, balance, industriousness, kindness, and good manners. If you and your child get involved in the sport, no doubt you will find things to add to this list!

Any Drawbacks?

Even though horse people sing the praises of riding most of the time, I would be remiss not to point out some potential drawbacks to the sport.

Like any activity that requires the development of skill to actually perform the activity to any extent, such as playing the piano, playing tennis, or skiing, learning how to ride takes time. Unless there is a horse stabled in a nearby backyard and a willing owner to help your child, the sport takes a certain commitment of not only time but money as well.

While it is certainly fun and recreational for you and your child to go to a hack barn where you can rent horses to ride on a trail from time to time, taking an occasional ride is about as instructive as taking an occasional piano lesson. No one will argue that such periodic exposure to one or the other doesn't have some merit, albeit mostly pleasure, but it would be a hard way to build up any skill. So, if your child wants to ride, offer to give her some lessons and plan to do it on a consistent basis. Once a week is a good way to start.

The sport has a reputation for being a rich person's sport. And it definitely *can* be. But put the emphasis on the word *can* because it does *not* have to be that way. There is plenty of opportunity for your child to ride on a modest budget, as long as you keep control and don't get pushed into anything beyond your means or good judgment.

Except for those lucky children who live next door to a stable, being able to ride is not as easy as opening the door and going out

First Considerations

For most families, the cost of riding—especially for recreational activities—is an important consideration. You want to know, even in general terms, what the price tag for horseback riding is going to be. Bearing in mind that costs can vary from area to area, and even within the same area (for lessons, for instance), and that there is definitely a price spread for apparel and equipment as well, I do my best to direct you to the information you need, with lists of tack dealers and other guides. In this sport, like anywhere else, it's a good idea to comparison shop, ask questions about what you're getting, look for deals (shopping online and through catalogs and by trying tactics such as paying for multiple lessons), and, when appropriate and to your liking, buy previously owned items.

to play ball in the yard or nearby playground. You or someone else has to chauffeur your child to and from the stable.

Yes, in all likelihood your youngster is going to get bumped and bruised somewhere along the way. Believe me, it happens to anyone who rides! This is, after all, a very physical sport. And there's no use denying the fact, either, that if your child takes a bad fall, she can get hurt. Even the smallest pony is a living creature weighing several times more than any child, and accidents do happen.

That said, most times mishaps are minor and far between. As parents find out very early on, children are amazingly resilient and break-proof. Just as they fall off bicycles, skis, and skateboards, most of them tumble off horses and get back on before you have time to say, "Are you all right?"

When to Begin?

Because *learning* how to ride takes some degree of concentration and coordination, between ages six and seven is usually a good time to begin the process. Children younger than this generally cannot control the situation either mentally or physically, and to expect them to do otherwise could lead to trouble.

However, by age four, and even sometimes at younger ages, if a child seems interested, she can be carefully introduced to the sport. Young children love to see and pet animals. Introducing them to a horse, just as you would to a dog or cat, can help them to develop sensitivity and understanding. At that age, you would not expect your youngster to actually begin learning any skills, but if she is put up on a pony and walked around on a lead line, with an instructor right beside her, it can be a safe, positive experience. And naturally, there are children who will surprise everyone by picking up the reins and the basics of the sport before you would ever expect them to do so.

Every instructor has an opinion about when a child is the right age to start riding. Some will agree to work with very young children, as long as the parent understands that, for the most part, the child will spend less time learning and more time having fun and becoming comfortable with a horse. Other instructors will simply not teach very young children. So, your child's age may be a factor in choosing your stable.

Before, or even a little after, age seven, the idea to ride is frequently the parent's idea. Perhaps you rode as a child, or wanted to, and now you would like to give that opportunity to your child. That's fine, as long as you remember that what can and cannot be accomplished depends on when your child starts.

By age eight or nine, children usually come up with the idea to ride by themselves, with no prompting from their parents. Telltale signs of an interest in riding can include turning over lawn furniture to make a jumping course, galloping around the living room, eating lots of carrots, or taping horse pictures to bedroom walls.

Age eight or nine is a good age to start. At this age, children have been in school for several years and have learned how to pay attention and absorb information. Their bodies have become stronger and more agile, and there is increasing mind-body coordination. In all, they are now better prepared both mentally and physically and most likely will take to riding more quickly and easily than younger children.

Getting Acquainted with Riding

Even if your child is the right age and is excited to begin riding, signing her up for a series of riding lessons may still seem like a big undertaking. You know she wants to ride, but you continue to drag your feet. After all, you see a mountain of problems. The stable is some distance from home. You will have to drive there, then wait around until the lesson is over. You don't know for sure, but she will probably need some special clothing or equipment. And then, what if she doesn't like it all that much? Not unreasonable concerns, to be sure.

So, before you take the big step, you might consider some alternate ways of getting acquainted with the sport. All are various "package deals" that can give you and your child a taste of horseback riding and what is involved, as well as a look at a particular stable, in a short-term, less committed way.

A number of youth organizations and programs for young people offer riding programs on a regular or periodic basis. Among them are the Boy Scouts, Girl Scouts (or Cub Scouts and Brownies, depending on your child's age), Police Athletic League, YMCA and YWCA, YMHA and YWHA, Boys and Girls Clubs, 4H, local church groups and other religious organizations, and schools. Also, in the summer, both day and sleepover camps often include riding as an available activity.

Such arrangements usually offer an organized group of children a lesson or two a week for a set number of weeks. The lesson will run anywhere from half an hour to an hour. If the group is larger than the number of horses available, half the children will ride at a time. Meanwhile, those waiting may go off to another part of the stable and get a lesson in horse and equipment care.

Since this would be a group of absolute beginners who have never ridden before, there should be several assistants besides the main instructor, perhaps even one for every horse and rider. And while a situation like this cannot provide your youngster with the

11

same intensity of instruction she would get from a private lesson, these short programs can be a fun, relaxed way for her to get a sense of what riding is like and perhaps whet her appetite for more.

A series of group lessons like this can also benefit you, the parent, by helping to convince you that riding will be a good activity for your child. You will have company among the others watching from the rail of the riding ring. You probably won't have to do all the chauffeuring, either, since that detail can get split up among several parents or maybe handled completely by others. However, if horses and your child don't mix, you will find this out, too, without a big investment of time and money

Another possibility that can help acquaint your child with riding is a program, usually held in the summer, offered by a stable itself. Children of different riding abilities, including first-time riders, can take a week or two of daylong instruction in riding and other facets of the sport. Such programs will probably include a couple hours of riding, one in the morning and another in the afternoon, plus hands-on experience in learning to take care of horses and equipment. Sometimes at the end of the session there is even a little competition, during which the children can show off how much they have learned and win ribbons to happily hang up at home.

What's Next?

If this first sampling of horseback riding leaves a nice afterglow, if your child keeps reminding you of this funny incident or that exciting day during her brief riding experience, you can be fairly sure that, at least from her standpoint, the light is green. And if you are at all inclined—and certainly, if she is pestering you—it is a good bet that it is worth taking the next step.

That next step is finding a stable where your child can continue taking lessons. Your journey into how and where to find that stable, how to judge what you're looking at—in terms of the facility, its horses, and its instructors—and how to put all the pieces together and set up your child's first lesson begins on the next page.

Chapter Two

First Steps Toward Riding

*I*f your youngster has tasted horseback riding, thanks to a youth program or other organizational arrangement, perhaps you have gotten past your initial discomfort. But maybe not. Even after the good things that have been said about horseback riding, you're still a little nervous. There, you've admitted it, and you are still reading! That's another step forward.

There are variations on this reluctance. Many people have had encounters with horses, frequently as children. They rode briefly, but because they were not supervised carefully or taught properly, the experience wasn't very good.

Maybe this was your story. Perhaps you had only taken three or four lessons when, one day, your instructor said, "See that crossrail? Trot over it. It's easy. Just lean forward and grab mane." Except for one thing: You hadn't had any preparation. The horse got a little quick and strong and took a bigger-than-expected jump. Your feet flew out of your stirrups, you lost your grip on his mane, and you sailed through the air, hitting the ground scared, shaken, and bruised.

Or when you were a beginning rider, maybe a careless instructor put you on a horse with a little too much energy. Something spooked him, and he ran away with you. And he kept running until, after many terror-filled seconds, you fell off in a heap, hitting the ground with such force that it literally knocked the wind out of you. Whatever the sad story, it has stayed in your memory and, understandably, makes it a little harder for you to let your child take up riding.

Before you close the door on the whole idea, consider a couple points. Think through those old memories as best you can, and chances are you will see that the mishap was probably a result of carelessness and could have been avoided. With this book as a guide, you will be able to create a better experience for your child, starting with finding a stable and an instructor whose first consideration is safety.

Finding a Stable

If you decide to get acquainted with riding through a youth group program or other "package" arrangement, and if you like the stable and instructor involved, you have probably found a place where your child can continue riding. However, you may have decided to forge ahead on your own. If so, now you need to find a stable.

What you're looking for is a stable with a riding program—not what is commonly called a hack barn, which routinely rents out most or all of its horses for group trail rides. While such operations serve a very worthwhile purpose in making horses available for people who just want to ride occasionally, unless the hack barn runs a separate boarder-and-lesson business, this is not the place for you.

So where is the stable you want? Stop and think about it for a minute; you may already know of one, maybe even a couple. Especially if you live in the suburbs or a rural area, chances are pretty good that there is one in your vicinity. Even in some cities— among them New York, Chicago, and Los Angeles—there are actually stables located within the city limits.

Then again, the word *stable* may draw a complete blank in your mind. Not only are you still shaking your head, wondering how your child came up with this whole idea, but now that you are willing to at least entertain the notion, where are you going to go?

Try networking. No doubt you've already used this tactic in business or elsewhere, and now it is just as likely to produce the whereabouts of a stable or two. Friends and relatives are a good starting point. Think back. Wasn't someone you know, or heard about, taking riding lessons a couple years ago? How about your youngster's classmates or friends in the neighborhood? Maybe one of them is actually taking lessons right now, which may well explain where your child's idea came from!

Ask other parents. In the bargain, you may find some who are also interested or whose children are interested in riding, too. Having company in a new undertaking is always reassuring. And besides, more parents can spread out the task of getting children to and from a stable, which lessens the wear and tear on everyone.

Then there are your telephone book's Yellow Pages. Look first under "stables" or "riding academies." If there are listings under either heading, these are the places that are most likely to have pleasure horses, probably a combination of some that are privately owned and boarded there and some that are owned by the stable and available for use in lessons. A stable may even run a box ad in the phone book, listing what it offers, which may include private and group lessons, a lighted indoor arena (as well as an outdoor one), and trail riding nearby.

Remember, however, that a business has to pay to be listed in the Yellow Pages, so even if "stables" or "riding academies" fails to produce what you are looking for, it doesn't mean that there aren't any in your area. It just means you are going to have to dig a little deeper. You can start by checking with allied businesses that may be able to direct you to a stable. For example, establishments under "riding apparel and equipment," "tack shops," "horse furnishings," and "saddlery and harness," if there are any listed, are selling their wares to people involved with horses; and "feed dealers" are selling feed to livestock owners, which may include horse owners. Of course, you can also search the Internet for stable locations, though chances are you will find only larger establishments. These may be to your liking, but at this early stage, don't overlook the small, well-run local stables that may not have Web sites.

If other avenues fail, look under "horses" for listings such as "dealers" and "training." These likely will lead you to buyers and sellers of racehorses and other sport horses before pleasure horse stables, but if nothing else works, it's another place to network. Horse people tend to know what is going on beyond their own little niche, and someone will almost certainly know of a stable.

A couple more thoughts: A local college may have an equestrian or riding team and practice at a stable in the vicinity. Call your local colleges to see if they have teams and where they ride. Teams have their own trainers, but the fact that they use a particular stable suggests that the facilities may be good. Also, keep watch over the classified ads in your local paper. As with anything else listed there, it's catch-as-catch-can. Riding stables might advertise, but for sure, people selling and buying horses do. Call up a prospective seller and ask where his horse is stabled or call a buyer to find out where she'll be going.

In a word, work all the angles. You never know where your best lead will come from and what riding connections you will make for the future!

Good Stables and Not So Good Ones

Just as there are good and bad versions of most things, there are good and bad stables. Some, after you are on the premises only a short time, will telegraph to you, loud and clear, "Get in your car and drive away." At others, it may take a little longer for you to see that this is not a place where you want your child to ride. Conversely, there are stables where all the pieces fit and you feel at home right from the start. Hopefully, this book will help you find that place.

Just because you are not a horse person who has grown up around these beautiful creatures does not mean that you will not be able to distinguish good from bad in the business. Have confidence in yourself. Your intuition and gut reactions are as valid here as they are anywhere else. Back these with an understanding of what to look for and what to expect, beginning with your first visit to the stable, and you will be able to find the right riding situation for your child.

Stables for Every Taste

Stables come in different sizes, styles, orientations, and combinations of all these things, from large to small; from fancy to laid-back, family-run operations; and from stables catering to one breed or discipline to melting pots with an assortment of horses and riders. Among them you can find one that will not only suit the personalities of you and your child but also your budget.

Realistically, however, in your area there may be several choices or just a couple, and thus there is a range in the number of variables to consider. Nevertheless, begin by keeping it simple. Note some basics that appeal to you and your child and use that as your first shopping list. First, is size a factor? Are you and your child both generally okay in larger, busier situations, with lots of activity going on, or would something smaller and probably quieter be a better choice? Do you gravitate toward polish and ambiance, or is something less fancy than that okay? Be open-minded but also honest with yourself because you don't want to start fretting from the moment you settle on a stable.

That said, of course, the choice you make can be temporary—a good place for your child to get her first taste of riding over the next six months to a year or however long she's comfortable there. Or you may find a stable that has the instructors and facilities to bring your child along over the next several years.

Big barns, as you would expect, generally have more of everything: more horses, more people around, and more riding facilities. They may house a hundred horses or more, most of them privately owned, some for sale. If the riding program is open to nonboarders, there will probably be a good number of outside participants and several school horses and instructors. Facilities may include a lighted indoor arena with a visitors' gallery in addition to several outdoor riding areas. Although not all stables fit these distinctions, small barns generally have fewer facilities, horses, and riders.

If a stable is known as a show barn, many of its riders regularly take their horses to horse shows. This would include students in the riding program, and you can expect that as soon as your child is ready, she will be encouraged to take one of the school horses to a show and you to let her. A barn like this caters to show riders, and it likes to see its riders, even the youngest ones, out there winning ribbons. This is a calling card for the barn's staff—a public demonstration of who they are and what they do. Certainly, the more horses and riders going to shows, the more attention they create. But being a show barn has less to do with size than with what a good number of the riders are focused on doing.

To the extent that choices are available in your area, size, level of activity, ambiance, and focus will all factor into what appeals to you and your child in a barn. Will being around others, especially children who already have their own horses and may be able to spend more money on the sport than you can or wish to, make you feel pressured and uncomfortable? (If it's a large barn, just by virtue of the numbers, you'll likely find some of that.) More so than adults, kids can be very impressionable and want what their peers have. However, can you reap the benefits of more, and perhaps better, facilities and shrug off the negatives?

With many stops in between, and many combinations of barn size, atmosphere, and types of riders, the other end of the spectrum might well be a small, much more relaxed-feeling stable, quite possibly family run. The horses here can be every bit as nice as those at a larger operation, but there are far fewer of them. There is probably only one riding ring—an outdoor one—but it likely has nice equipment. Some of the riders go to shows, and quite regularly, but there is no feeling that you aren't "one of them" if you don't want to do the same. In all, small barns give you a close-knit feeling, sort of like what you'd get at a small school.

Calling Stables

After you have tossed around the pros and cons of horseback riding, with the pros winning enough votes for you to seek out one or more stables, it is time to start telephoning to decide which ones are worth a visit.

People who work at stables are generally on the job soon after sunrise, feeding and watering the horses and beginning their daily chores. To give them a chance to start their day, don't call until after nine o'clock. If the stable is large enough to have a front office, chances are no one will be at the desk until then, anyway.

If necessary, let the phone ring a good long time. Even small stables are spread out, and if someone is at the other end of the riding ring, it can take several minutes to get to the phone. Be patient. You may be calling the stable that will be perfect for your child.

When you reach someone, be simple and direct, "Do you give lessons?" The answer will be either "Yes, we do" or "No, this is strictly a boarding barn." If the latter, it means that all the horses are privately owned and any instruction that is given is only to the owner or designated rider of a particular horse. There are no horses that are owned by the management and available for use in lessons for nonboarders.

If the answer is "Yes," you should next ask, "Do you teach children, and how old must they be to start riding?" Also, at this time you can ask what the fees are for private and group lessons. Then, assuming that your child meets the minimum age requirement, if there is one, and if the fees are within your budget, find out when it would be convenient to visit the stable.

Types of Lessons

Riding lessons come in three varieties: private, semiprivate, and group lessons. Just about any stable will offer private and group lessons. Semiprivate ones may be available in theory, but the actuality depends on two riders of like ability being available to ride at the same time.

The cost of lessons varies quite a bit in different parts of the United States, but you can expect to pay about the same price as for other sports instruction, like tennis and skiing lessons, in your area. But still, some comparison shopping is in order; even in the same area, the same price, especially for private lessons, may bring different amounts of riding time. (And to be sure, each stable will tell you its approach is best.)

Shop around and don't be shy about asking what you get for your lesson dollars. Stables frequently offer a reduced rate, maybe the cost of one lesson, if you buy a series of lessons rather than purchase them one at a time. For instance, you might get ten lessons for the price of nine. You probably don't want to purchase such a package before the first lesson, but it's something to keep in mind. To the extent that the cost of horseback riding is an important factor for you, weighing prices may influence your choice of a stable.

Private lessons, when your child will have the instructor's undivided attention, are the most expensive. Depending on a stable's policy, they may be taken for an hour or a half hour. No matter what type of lessons you decide on later, your child's first lesson will be private, probably a half hour in length. Some of that will be what is called ground time, when she is introduced to her horse and becomes comfortable standing beside him before she gets on his back. Of course, if she has already had a few lessons (as part of a riding package given by some organization), she may be impatient to move things along and get in the saddle sooner!

Semiprivate lessons, when two children share a time slot, are usually only offered in one length—an hour or thereabouts. They may be an option if your child and another youngster want to pair up together or if you specifically ask the instructor whether another beginning rider would be interested in riding with your child. Likewise, the instructor, with another student in mind, may suggest the same. Semiprivates can be a good, middle-of-the-road solution that saves you a few dollars and still provides a good amount of one-on-one attention.

Group lessons, when the instructor divides his attention among several children, are the least expensive. Even in a group lesson, a good instructor will still be able to critique individual riders directly. Though of necessity they lack much one-on-one instruction, group lessons make up for that by being a great deal of fun for young riders, who respond to one another's energy and enthusiasm and learn a lot by watching one another ride.

Larger stables with active riding programs will have more instructors and more school horses than smaller stables, but barn size itself won't decide how many riders will be in a group lesson. A lesson in any barn should be no more than five or six students. It could be fewer, depending on how many youngsters are beginning riding at the same time. Having more instructors can mean that the barn has smaller classes, but so can having fewer students at a particular level. However, if you're told the group will have ten, twelve, or more riders, the class is going to be a lot more about exercise than learning, so you'd best look elsewhere.

Be up front with your questions. Along with asking the price and whether the stable gives lessons to children, find out what types of lessons are offered, their length, and the maximum number of riders in a group lesson. It shows you're doing your homework.

Checking Out the Stable

Before you actually visit the stable or stables that sound promising, think a little about what you need to find out. While you don't want to come across as a know-it-all, it's helpful to sound like you have some idea of what you are talking about.

If you feel unsure of yourself, bring a friend along, especially one who has ridden before. It is reassuring to have company in an unfamiliar setting, and it's helpful to have another pair of eyes. Also, your friend may remember to ask a question or two that you have forgotten.

Stables are not like tennis courts or rolling lawns, places you can stroll about easily. They are rough-hewn places, so to speak, not unlike barnyards in the amount of dirt and mud that's about. So, dress comfortably, with particular attention to your shoes. No thin heels, please, and no open-toed sandals! Wear comfortable, flat shoes that will not be ruined if some mud or manure gets stuck to them.

You will want to talk with someone in charge, preferably the owner, manager, or head instructor. Depending on the size of the stable, these may be different people or just one person. Expect them to be friendly and willing to talk, though not so anxious that they will leave a student in the middle of a lesson, other than to say, "Hello, I'll be with you in a few minutes." However, if they are brusque or too busy to talk with you at all, there is undoubtedly another stable where you will find people who do have time for you. You are visiting a stable to decide whether this is a good place for your child to learn how to ride, and the people there should make you feel confident that you have found the right place.

Ask if it is okay to walk around. The barn and surrounding areas should look cared for. With horses in residence, it is impossible to have a barn that is spotless, but "picked up" is another matter. Piles of manure left where they drop and debris in places where people and horses can trip over it doesn't speak well.

Take a good look at the horses as you walk through the barn. Are they bright-eyed, with healthy-looking, glossy coats? Do they seem well fed, or are their ribs showing? Do they have an alert, interested attitude, or are they sulking in the backs of their stalls? Do they seem relaxed, or do they act jumpy? Do they look like they are routinely groomed, or do they have dull, dirty coats, maybe with mud caked to them, that probably haven't been brushed in a while? How are the stalls? Do they look freshly mucked, or as if they haven't been cleaned in a couple of days? How people treat their horses says volumes about the people themselves, the kind of operation they run, and how they will treat your child.

Exercise a little caution as you move about, and ask if it is all right to pet the horses before you do so. There might be one who tries to bite, especially when people are abrupt and appear threatening in their movements. Treat the horses gently.

After you have looked over the stable as a whole, you'll want to ask specifically about the school horses. These are the ones that the stable itself owns or uses for lessons through special arrangements with other owners. Ask to see them. They should look as healthy and cared for as any private horse in the barn.

How many school horses are there? If lessons are given regularly, a stable should have several for riders of different abilities, including a couple for absolute beginners. Are the horses regularly turned out into a paddock or pasture to run, play, and relax? (Yes, they definitely should be, for some portion of every day.)

Are they schooled by more advanced riders to keep them from developing bad habits that beginning riders cannot handle? (Yes to this, too.) Approximately how many hours a day is each horse used? (A couple hours a day, with time off between lessons to relax, is best. Of course, there will be extenuating circumstances at times, such as one of the other school horses being lame. But overall, they should be very well treated.) Are they used for lessons every day, or do they get days off? (They should get days off, just like everyone else.)

School horses are, as a group, savvy, unflappable horses who are kind and gentle with beginners, forgiving of mistakes, and responsive to a rider's improvements. They come in all ages, sizes, colors, and breeds, and youngsters fall in love with them with predictable regularity. Good ones are worth their weight in gold and should be treated accordingly.

Check the stable's policy regarding cancellations. How much advance notice is required? Will you be charged for a lesson if you don't comply? What about inclement weather? Obviously, if it is raining and there is no indoor arena, your child won't be having a lesson. But what if it rained earlier and the riding ring is still very muddy? Will the stable call you to cancel, or are you expected to call? Or, as long as it is not actually raining by lesson time, does the stable expect you to show up?

Finally, ask if the stable carries liability insurance. Reputable stables do. As the parent or guardian of a minor, you should be asked to sign a form stating that you assume the risks to your child from riding.

Meeting the Instructor

Eventually, you will find a stable that feels comfortable, where the horses seem like a happy, healthy bunch. The people you have talked with there should be pleasant and accommodating, willing to spend time with you and answer your questions without making you feel like you are asking too many. At this point, it's time to get specific and talk about the stable's lesson program to decide if it is one your child can fit into.

English or Western?

Now that you know about English and Western or, more precisely, English hunt seat and Western stock seat, the two most popular riding disciplines, you may be wondering whether your child has a choice as to which one she learns.

Well, yes and no. Certainly, if you feel strongly about one style over the other, you can make a concerted effort to find a stable that focuses on the one you prefer. If you don't have a preference, where you live will help to decide what your child learns. Western, as the name suggests, is more popular in the United States in the Southwest and West; English is prevalent on the East Coast of the United States, Great Britain, and Europe. That said, however, in the United States you will find plenty of English riding in the West and Western riding in the East. There is also, in some parts of the United States, a fondness for English saddle seat and riding high-stepping three-gaited and five-gaited Saddlebred horses. In fact, if you look hard enough, you will find a little bit of everything almost everywhere.

Of course, after a person rides for a while, he or she tends to develop an affinity for one style over another and gravitate toward it. I, for instance, ride English, with an occasional turn in a Western saddle. And while I'm familiar with other styles, it has largely been through conversation and observation.

English riding is considered the sport seat, a discipline that can lead to such later pursuits as riding hunters and jumpers

To repeat, lessons can be offered in three ways: private lessons, when the instructor teaches only one child at a time; semiprivate lessons, when two children are taught at the same time; and group lessons, when from three to a maximum of six children are taught together. Stables may or may not offer all three types, and instructors have their preferences as to what they teach, too.

over obstacles in a show ring, fox hunting, and, for women, riding sidesaddle. English tack, especially the saddle, is lighter and more pared down than its Western counterpart. The rider's formal attire, from high boots to formfitting breeches and tailored jacket, harks back to the dress of English squires in the eighteenth and nineteenth centuries.

Historically, Western-style riding is the working seat, still used by ranch hands and wranglers today, who must ride for hours on end, moving cattle herds. The bigger saddle is easily recognized by its metal horn at the front end, around which the cowboy tosses a coiled lasso, and the heavy, tooled leather of which the saddle is made. As you would expect, this is a comfortable seat for trail riding.

Western riders train and compete with their horses, as do their English riding counterparts, though rodeos and other Western competitions bear the stamp and flair of the Old West.

Regardless of the seat, the horse is the same. True, different breeds are favored by different schools of riding, and they are trained differently and asked to perform in somewhat different ways by more proficient riders. And like riders, horses perform best in the way they're trained and ridden most frequently. Some can switch from English to Western with relative ease, but most don't. It takes some retooling! Nevertheless, all horses walk, trot, canter, and gallop; eat grain and hay; drink gallons of water; and respond to love and kindness.

Now you would like to meet the instructor who teaches them. Riding instructors, just like other teachers, have strengths and weaknesses. Some specialize in starting young children and then move them on to other instructors as they get older and improve. Others will only work with older, more advanced riders.

Don't listen only to an instructor's accomplishments with other riders, such as how many regularly go to horse shows or

Finding a Certified Instructor

If you want your child to ride with a certified instructor, check these Web sites to find one in your area:

American Riding Instructors Association (ARIA)
www.riding-instructor.com
239-948-3232

Certified Horsemanship Association (CHA)
www.cha-ahse.org
800-399-0138

have qualified for year-end awards. That is impressive, to be sure, but it is future talk. Perhaps it will be important to you some day, but right now you need only one thing: an instructor who has experience working with young children and is successful in teaching them how to ride.

There is a growing interest in the United States in seeing that instructors carry certification from the American Riding Instructors Association (ARIA) or another national organization. In addition, some states require instructors to be licensed. While these are facts separate from how much you like an instructor's teaching style, when held, credentials do speak to a baseline of competence.

If finding a certified instructor for your child gives you some measure of security, then that is certainly a good approach. In so doing, you will know that a board of his peers has deemed your child's instructor capable of teaching in specific disciplines and at specific levels. In your case, that would include teaching beginners.

Because certification involves some hefty fees, however, you should keep in mind that there are many capable, talented instructors who are not certified, for whatever reason, financial or other. It's also very possible that a certified instructor is not available in your area.

Whatever you decide regarding certification, you should still take time to question the prospective instructor about his or her experience (though remember, from here on this book assumes that the instructor is male), particularly if he is young. There are no right answers, but here are some things that can help you with your decision: How long has the instructor been teaching, especially children? (Obviously, age has to do with how long he's been doing this, but you don't want your child to be one of his first students, either. Look for some experience.) How long has he been at that stable? (If he's new there, you may want to talk to stable management to get a sense of him from them.) How many lessons a week does he teach? (This can be tricky because instructors earn money per lesson so, naturally, they want to teach a fair amount. But hopefully, a full schedule indicates that they're well regarded, not that the stable is short on instructors! You'll have to sort through the answers.) How long has he been riding? (Again, experience counts. You don't want to hear that someone who is a relatively new rider is now teaching.) Simply put, you want your child to be taught by someone who has been around for a while, who has coped with a variety of students and situations, and whom riders choose to study with.

Your reaction to a riding instructor after a short meeting, while subjective, of course, is certainly as valid as your reaction to your child's grade school teacher. You want someone who makes you feel comfortable and gives you the sense that your child is going to be well cared for.

He is a teacher just like any other, and he ought to be able to explain things in simple, understandable terms. If the answers to your questions are vague, lofty, or evasive, find another instructor. If you cannot understand his answers, how in the world will he be able to explain things to your child? A good teacher has the patience and imagination to make himself understood.

If he does this, ask when he is going to be teaching some youngsters, and if it would be all right for you to watch him for a little while. If a lesson isn't in the offing, come back another day; meanwhile, you can think about what you've seen and remember some of the questions you forgot to ask.

When you return, bring your child along, if possible. Let her meet the instructor and watch a lesson with you. Children frequently have strong reactions to people. It's better to find out now whether this is someone she would like to take lessons from or whether she thinks he's a mean old grump or other unsavory type.

In watching a lesson, do a little projecting yourself: Will your child get along well with this person? Does he have a good rapport with the children he is teaching? Do they seem to like him? Do they listen to him? Are they having fun? Does he give them his undivided attention, or does he get distracted by things going on elsewhere?

How does the instructor handle a difficult situation, such as a horse who doesn't want to move or a child who gets upset? Is he kind and patient, or does he lose his temper and raise his voice?

Where is the lesson being given? Children, especially beginning riders, whether alone or in a group, should be taught in a small, enclosed area such as a fenced-in outdoor ring or a portion of an indoor arena. Letting youngsters ride in a large area, even if it is enclosed, invites trouble because a horse who is going to bolt and run away with a rider is more likely to do so where there is a lot of space.

Are the children alone in the ring, or are other riders also there? If the latter, are they riding quietly, being careful not to distract the children, or are they being pushy and inconsiderate? Is this the only lesson going on, or is another instructor teaching at the same time? In a stable with privately owned horses, unless there are other places to ride, it is difficult to reserve a ring just for a lesson. However, if there are other riders, the situation should be handled in a way that is safe for all.

Special Considerations for Your Child

If there are some things about your child that would be helpful for the instructor to know in working with her, or if there is a medical condition that he should be aware of, don't hesitate to say something. Speak to him privately, not in front of your child or others at the stable. But, easy now. It may be that you are a little nervous and the dozen things that just came to mind are more than you need to lay on the instructor all at once. Select a couple—and only if they are important.

To be sure, you need to point out some things, just as you would to a teacher at school. You should mention if your child has diabetes, asthma, or another medical condition; if she is unusually timid or retiring; or if she has a disability, be it physical, mental, or emotional, that is not immediately apparent (and not one that would require her to be in a special riding program, about which you'll learn more in the appendix).

While you are not looking to overplay anything and create restrictions and limitations for your child, other than what may be absolutely necessary for her health and well-being, informing the instructor may help him to steer a path around something that could become a roadblock. Whatever your concerns, giving the instructor a heads-up may save your child from being singled out and embarrassed, and nobody else need be any the wiser.

Scheduling the First Lesson

With all your immediate questions answered, when you feel comfortable with a stable and an instructor, you can start by signing up for one half-hour lesson. Even if, should your child continue, you plan for her to take semiprivate or group lessons either for budget reasons or because you think it will be a better arrangement for her, most instructors will recommend that the first one be private. In fact, stable management may well insist on it. For a number of reasons, this short private time gives everyone involved the best chance to see what's in store.

A half hour is a sufficiently long time to ask a youngster to focus her mind and body on something new, without getting sore muscles and mentally fatigued! It is also enough time for you both to start to relax and feel comfortable around a horse—and for you to feel more secure in the knowledge that you are not getting your child into something that is going to frighten her or get her hurt. Quite the opposite: When handled with care and sensitivity, this first lesson will pave the way for many more.

Chapter Three

The First Lesson

*I*f you arrive a little early for your child's first lesson, you and your child can relax and take a few minutes to watch what's going on around the stable. This will also give you a chance to remind the instructor, in case some time has passed since your last meeting, of your child's age and the fact that this is her first riding lesson.

This lesson should be held in a small, enclosed area. The horse she will ride should also be one of the stable's gentlest school horses, a real babysitter who will take care of her, even if she is a little timid or uncertain.

The instructor will do his best to pair your child with the most suitable horse. If she is small, her mount for this lesson may actually be a small pony. If she is a little bigger in size, she may be riding a larger pony or a small horse. In any case, this horse should be patient, kind, docile, forbearing, and forgiving. The last thing your child needs is to be frightened by an animal who is too big and seems to have too much energy. As the instructor comes over to greet you and introduce your child to her first horse, hopefully you will get the feeling that she is about to make a new friend.

What to Wear

There are three items to pay particular attention to in deciding what your child should wear for her first lesson: shoes, pants, and a riding hat.

For riding, even at the very beginning, your child should wear shoes that are sturdy, with a hard sole, a hard toe, and a definite heel. The hard sole will let her foot slide in and out of the stirrup, an important safety feature. The hard toe protects the foot, just in case a horse steps on it (yes, such things do happen), and the heel keeps the foot from sliding all the way through the stirrup and getting caught. Given today's fashions, a pair of street shoes— oxford types or short boots—with chunky heels may already be in your child's closet.

Sneakers are a bad choice. The rubber sole, especially with the deep crevices that many of them have, can get caught on the stirrup. The soft toe offers no real protection, and there is no heel to stop the foot from accidentally sliding all the way through the stirrup.

Your child's pants should be long enough that her bare legs don't get rubbed raw by the stirrup leathers or saddle. Jeans or corduroys are a good choice, but they should not be so tight that welt seams cause irritating marks. Sweatpants and Lycra tights are not good ideas because they tend to be slippery, and your child will slide around in the saddle even more than she is likely to do at first, anyway.

The third item of clothing that is an absolute must is a riding hat, also referred to as a schooling helmet, with a strap that fastens under the chin. Check beforehand to make sure, but most stables will provide one for your child's use, at least for the first few lessons. A riding hat will protect her head during a fall, and no child should be allowed to ride a horse without one.

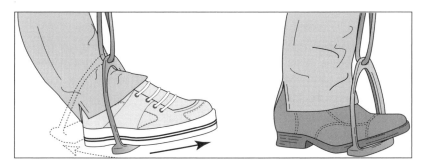

(a) Incorrect: Sneaker, with no heel, sliding through stirrup. (b) Correct: Boot resting properly in stirrup.

The stable's hat, of course, will have been used by other young-sters and will no doubt be well worn and maybe a little scruffy. If that bothers you, arrange to buy your own before the first lesson (from a tack shop, riding supply catalog, or online source; see the sidebar "Tack Shops to Get You Started" in chapter 4 for a few good places and the sidebar "Tack Suppliers" in chapter 5 for more sources). But if you can relax about a little dirt, which you will see on her a lot more if she continues riding, why not let the stable supply the hat, at least until you are sure your child is going to like this new endeavor?

If the weather is chilly, your child will probably be adding out-erwear, like a jacket or heavy sweater. In this case, see that she chooses something comfortable that allows for plenty of upper body movement. You don't want any of her clothing to be too snug and restricting. However, don't let her wear something too bulky or oversized because then the instructor won't be able to see her body position. And just like any other time you send your youngster out to play, make sure what she is wearing is washable and not brand new.

Should You Watch?

Whether or not you watch this first lesson won't make any differ-ence to the instructor. In fact, he will undoubtedly be happy to have you do so, as long as your presence doesn't distract your child or in any other way hinder the lesson. For her well-being, it is important for the instructor to have your child's full attention.

You will be asked to stand outside the ring, along the rail, or in some other spot out of the way of other horses and riders mov-ing about. Sometimes indoor arenas have visitors' galleries, where you can sit and watch the lesson from behind a Plexiglas window.

The question really is: How do you and your child feel about you watching the lesson? Is it something you want to do, or does this new venture still make you a bit nervous? Will your being close by give your child extra confidence, or does she really want to "do it alone" without you right there? How would you handle another type of lesson? Would you watch a tennis lesson or sit in the back of the room during a piano lesson? "Well, this is different," you say. "There's a horse. . . . " True, there *is* a horse, who is also helping to teach your child. But how different is that, really? It's still a lesson.

Of no help to anyone is a parent who hovers at the rail, visibly nervous and jumpy in anticipation that rider, horse, or instructor will make the slightest wrong move, real or imagined. Despite her best intentions, this parent has never quite reconciled the idea of her child riding a horse, and now that it is happening, she is clearly uncomfortable. The trouble is, without meaning to, she will transfer this anxiety to her child, making it harder for her to learn.

You'll be more helpful to all if you're an enthusiastic parent, watching the lesson in a relaxed manner, pleased that your child is learning something new. If you think you'll be too nervous to do that, watch for a few minutes and then take a stroll through the barn or chat with some of the other people around. When you reappear, you will probably be pleased to see that your child is having a good time and getting along quite well.

And oh, yes, be sure you are dressed comfortably for standing around. A half hour can crawl by mighty slowly if your feet hurt or you are getting cold. Remember that this is a stable, where you need to wear shoes that won't be ruined if they get dirty!

What to Expect at the First Lesson

Every instructor has his own way of introducing a youngster to riding. While the game plan—to make the child comfortable, keep her interested, make it fun, and keep her safe—is essentially the same no matter where you ride, it is always subject to change. After all, every child is different, and a good instructor is perceptive enough to adjust his approach to each new situation. This first lesson will probably be a private lesson, about a half hour in length. It is essentially an evaluation lesson that will give the instructor a sense of how your child will take to horseback riding.

The first lesson will probably start with a little groundwork. Your child will get to meet her new horse or pony face to face, pet him, and spend a few minutes standing beside him, perhaps learning a little about the bridle and saddle the horse is wearing. This part of the lesson should be kept very low key, much like getting to know a new dog or cat.

If your child seems uneasy, she, the horse, and the instructor may go for a little walk around a portion of the ring. Then if she starts to relax and sees that the horse is a new friend and companion, your child may feel ready to sit on the horse's back. Of course, if the child has been the one who has wanted to ride all along, she may want to curtail the pleasantries and mount up right away!

Many instructors will keep control of a new rider by snapping a lead line to one side of the horse's bridle and holding the other end. The child has the reins in her hands and feels as if she is riding, but the instructor also has hold of the horse so that he cannot wander off.

The lead line is sort of like training wheels on a bicycle. It gives the child a sense of security (since she doesn't know how to steer yet), but at the same time allows her to try to make the horse do things. The lead line is an important safety precaution, although wandering off is probably the furthest thing from this trusted school horse's mind. He has taken care of many beginning riders, and until your child learns a little more, the only thing he will do is walk and stop on command.

Even if your child pulls on his mouth with a loud "Whoa" and then flaps the reins wildly and bangs her legs, yelling "Giddyap," this fine fellow is going to do just what he is supposed to do. And that, in all probability on this first day of riding, is to go no faster than a walk.

In this first lesson, your child is likely to learn how to get on the horse, hold the reins correctly, and shorten them as needed. While standing still, she may learn how to steer the horse left and right by gently pulling on the left rein and then the right. Then, under the control of the instructor, and likely still with the horse attached to a lead line, she will probably walk a short distance and then halt, several times.

Perhaps at the end of the lessons, if she looks relaxed and comfortable in the saddle, the instructor may run beside the horse, a hand on the reins, and let your child trot or jog a dozen strides or so.

Beyond the mechanics of a first lesson, though, what you should see is an instructor who seems to enjoy working with your child. You should sense some rapport beginning between the two of them, and your child should obviously be having a good time. And when it is over and you ask her how it was, hopefully, you will get an answer like, "Oh, boy, it was great! I want to do it again!"

Spotting a Poor Lesson or Instructor

Poor lessons taught by poor instructors are, fortunately or unfortunately, pretty easy to spot. Remember: You know your child, and you know when things are not right. If you see that she is frightened and cannot seem to get a grip on herself, is upset, or is bored, the lesson is not going well.

If your child is frightened, is it because she has been put on a horse that is too big and seemingly full of energy and intimidates her? Did he start to jog off the moment your child was in the saddle, making her bounce around and feel totally helpless and insecure?

Was the instructor impatient with her fearfulness, suggesting that she was "too big" to act like that? Did he raise his voice and bully her, telling her to do things without trying to explain, in the simplest terms, why he was asking her to do something? Did the instructor's careless, insensitive behavior seem to upset your child, perhaps even make her cry? An answer of "yes" to any of these questions sends a clear signal that you need to find another instructor. You want riding, especially for a beginning youngster, to be totally enjoyable. (Much later you can put up with grumbles after a difficult lesson!) Especially at the start, negative behavior aimed at your child can quickly cancel out the pleasure.

By contrast, did your child seem bored with the lesson? Was the instructor inattentive to her, turning away to chat with others in the ring? Worse yet, did he walk away, if only for a couple of minutes, leaving your child sitting alone on her horse, waiting? Did you see her looking around the ring, rather than listening to what the instructor was saying? Did she finally say something pointed like, "I want to get off"? Again, this is not the situation you should be looking for. If the instructor can't hold your child's attention and interest, little will get accomplished, and what, then, is the point?

After the lesson was over and you asked her how it went, did you get a shrug and a half-hearted, "Okay, I guess," instead of the enthusiastic response you were hoping for? True, you can read your child better than anyone, and maybe a low-key response is par for the course at this point in a new activity. Maybe your sense tells you it will improve. Or maybe this is her way of telling you she doesn't want to do this again, at least not with this instructor. You need to listen not only to what your child says but how she says it.

How Much Can You Judge from One Lesson?

What you can judge from one lesson comes down to this: If your child wants to come back and do it again, it was a success, at least from her standpoint.

What the first lesson accomplished in terms of riding progress was probably minimal, and that is all you can expect. It should have given your child a little confidence that she could make the horse do what she asked him to do.

The first lesson is much too early to tell anything about most youngsters' riding ability. It usually takes a few lessons to see how fast a child begins to pick things up. Then again, children learn at different rates, so don't compare your child to another. That isn't fair. Some are quick learners initially and then reach a plateau. Others are slow to start but later seem to grasp things much faster.

And how about you? What do you think of this first lesson? After doing so much up-front work—visiting the stable, talking with people in charge, observing a lesson—did it meet your expectations? Are you pleased with the instructor? Were the safety precautions what you thought they should be?

Perhaps now that you have seen a little more of the stable and watched your child taking a lesson, you have some second thoughts. Was the instructor who taught your child different from the one you expected to have? If so, were you given a reasonable explanation for the change and asked if it was all right? Or were you told that your child would be taught by whoever was available, without any further explanation?

Was there more commotion in the ring than there was when you watched the other lesson, and were some of the other riders less considerate of your child's lesson than they should have been? Bear in mind, during a lesson on a weekend, there will always be more ring traffic than during the week. Nevertheless, your child must still feel safe and secure.

Nothing is written in stone. If you are truly unhappy with the experience you and your child have just had, you can find another stable. That's why you began by paying for only one lesson. Then again, before you start searching anew and spending more time and energy, maybe it is worth telling the manager how you feel. After all, this could have been an unusual situation and one that can be corrected. So, if you have the patience and it wasn't a truly terrible experience, try a second lesson before you make up your mind one way or the other.

The same advice holds true if a child is timid about riding and comes away from the first lesson unhappy and still very nervous about the whole thing. This is especially true if riding is really being encouraged by the parent and the child is agreeing to it but without much self-confidence. Here, too, unless your child absolutely rejects the idea, try a second lesson. However, if she doesn't want to ride again after that, let it go for the time being and realize that it's just not the right time. Maybe another time will be better.

Above all, keep in mind that getting involved in riding should be something that you and your child choose to do. And for it to work, it has to be enjoyable. As with any other relationship, there is only so much you can deduce initially about a stable, but do your best to select one that gives you a good, positive feeling.

Chapter Four

Continuing with Riding

*A*s long as you and your child are pleased with the first lesson, essentially the decision to go on has been made. So, if you haven't done so yet, now is the time to make a game plan. Will your child take one lesson a week, or is one every other week what you can afford in terms of time and money? Are you considering a series of, perhaps, ten lessons, after which you will take another look at the whole situation? Or are you inclined toward a more casual "Let's just start taking lessons and see what happens" approach?

In learning how to ride, as in learning anything new, the more consistent the lessons, the faster the progress. If you can manage it, a lesson a week is a good pace for a beginning rider. For starters, the instructor may suggest two or three more private lessons, which can help your child begin to build a foundation, at the same time allowing her to express any fears and awkwardness without the embarrassment of others watching. Before you and the instructor make any decisions about what type of lessons your child will continue with for the longer term, particularly if your thought is that she should ride with a group, the instructor will want to make sure that your child is secure enough on a horse to hold her own in that sort of situation. And having a few more private lessons may be the best way for her to pick up the rudiments of riding that she will need before making any changes.

Some kids catch on to the basics almost immediately; others take a little time to build their level of confidence. But after the first lessons, you can make a choice as to how best to continue. As noted earlier, private lessons provide the most concentrated form of instruction. Your child will be the center of attention, and the lesson will be all about her learning how to ride. If you can afford them, and if your child likes the idea, there's little to debate: Go for it.

However, the other options have much to recommend them, not only to save you money but also because they provide the camaraderie and fun of riding with others. Whether semiprivate lessons can be arranged depends on the instructor or you knowing about another beginning rider about the same age as your youngster who might be interested in that arrangement and who is taking lessons at the same stable. As long as the two riders are compatible in a semiprivate lesson, the instructor will still be able to give each rider a great deal of attention.

Kids can learn a great deal by watching each other. When the other rider catches on to something first, it can provide that extra little push that helps your child improve more quickly, too. That's why the third option, group lessons, can be just the ticket for many youngsters. Certainly, it's the budget-conscious way to go, but it can also be lots of fun. If your child is gregarious, or even if she's a bit shy but willing, group lessons are a perfect way to get to know some of the other youngsters at the barn. Remember: Check to make sure the group your child will ride in is small. (Six or seven students should be tops, and fewer is better.)

Of course, ask the instructor what type of lessons he thinks will be workable. He won't know your child very well at this juncture, but he's taught lots of other children before her and should be a pretty good judge of children in general and how they'll fit in. You can always adjust things as you go along, slotting in a private lesson now and then, if your child needs extra help mastering some particular aspect of riding that's giving her trouble. But that's for later.

The First Few Lessons

Learning to ride a horse is unlike anything else your child has ever attempted. She is going to be asked to use muscles for new tasks and coordinate them in ways that she has never done before. And make no mistake, she is likely to be a little ouchy the next day! Fortunately for children, they are seldom deterred by things that adults *know* are difficult. Have you ever seen the way many children take to downhill skiing? Whatever the challenge, most of them jump right in and, if they like it, keep plugging away until they can do whatever is asked of them.

Nevertheless, it will take time, and you, watching from the sidelines, need to be patient and supportive. Your child has to learn how to keep her balance in the saddle while the horse is moving, at the same time using her legs, hands, and seat independently, and coordinating them all together. It will just barely begin to happen in the first few lessons, but that is the direction she is headed. With the right instructor to help her understand what is expected of her, your child will keep trying. And as she keeps trying, the instructor should compliment her achievements while always inching her ahead toward new challenges.

Some people liken riding a horse to riding a bicycle. With both, you must balance using your seat and legs, resting your feet in the stirrups or on the pedals, while your hands work separately. You must also learn to control what you are riding, at the same time being conscious of other riders and your surroundings.

As your child learns the "language" of riding, she and her horse will start to understand each other, and she will begin to actually handle him and make him do what she wants. Your child will learn that a kick, later refined to a squeeze, will make the horse move forward and that when she sits deep in the saddle and pulls back on the reins, the horse will stop. She will learn that when she pulls the right rein, the horse will turn right, and vice versa. And so begins this business of riding.

Your child will probably ride the same horse for at least the first few lessons. Children become attached to horses and look forward to riding "their" horse. If your child does well on a particular horse, it can help build confidence, and the instructor will likely keep them paired up. But it is a judgment call, and the instructor's sense of an especially bold youngster may be that letting her try different horses is a good tool to help her learn that each one is a little different. And seeing other horses in the ring, she may be curious to try them herself.

One thing is for sure: Whether she rides her "special" horse or switches around, your child will be on a wonderful school horse who has seen it all. Patiently and kindly, he will help yet another youngster learn how to ride, ignoring mistakes and probably saying to himself, "Hang in there, kid. You'll catch on one of these days!"

During the early lessons, your child should also begin learning about the equipment she is using, including how to position the saddle on the horse's back, tighten the girth, and put on the bridle. She will certainly need the instructor's helping hand through all of this, but she should start to become familiar with the steps involved in getting a horse ready to ride. She should also be taught the basics of safety with horses, both in handling them directly and in moving around them.

While this will give you a very general idea of what the early lessons should cover, it is unrealistic to attach a schedule to progress. Some children are natural-born riders and learn very quickly. Others are slower to progress but down the road will catch up and be just as good as faster learners. Each child will move according to a different timetable. One thing is certain, though: Progress will be enhanced by a good partnership between rider and instructor. The better they work together, the better rider your child will become.

One last development that, hopefully, will come with these first few lessons is your child's growing enthusiasm. She will begin to make new friends and hardly be able to wait for her next lesson. Then you will really know that you are on to something good!

Posting

During one of the early lessons, your child will make her first big breakthrough. "I learned how to post today," she will rush to tell you. "My instructor says it is one of the hardest things I will ever have to learn." Thrilled as you are about this exciting achievement, you are also madly trying to figure out what she just told you. Guess what? You have just had your first taste of a whole new vocabulary!

If your child is taking English-style riding lessons, you are going to hear a lot about posting, so a short explanation of what it is and does will be useful. Posting is what riders are doing when they rhythmically rise up and down in the saddle as the horse trots along. A rider posts to avoid bouncing in the saddle with the horse's every footfall.

The posting movement is actually initiated by the horse, whose upward bounce pushes the rider out of the saddle. After waiting a beat, the rider lowers her body back down to a light contact with the saddle, controlling her motion rather than letting herself bounce back down, and the cycle begins again. However, a beginning rider can't yet feel the horse's motion to take advantage of it, so at first she must force herself to rise out of the saddle and come back down. But soon enough it becomes an automatic act.

Herein lies the basic difference between the riding styles. Generally, stock seat riders on Western-broke horses don't post but instead do a sitting trot. By relaxing their seat and sitting deep in the saddle, they are able to sit smoothly through every motion. (Posting for Western riders is more

The Right Horse—or Pony—for Your Child

A good instructor has an instinct for pairing the right horse with the right rider. He knows his school horses from watching them accepted than it used to be, and you will see it done, even at shows. But traditionally, Western riders sit the trot, or jog, as they call it.)

By now you are certainly proud of your child's accomplishment. And you can see how difficult it is to post. But you are still wondering to yourself, "What does it do?" Basically, posting makes it more comfortable to ride a horse at a trot, which can be a jarring gait. It also helps the horse to move forward more easily. When the rider rises at the correct moment, she "unweights," or takes the weight off the shoulder that the horse is getting ready to lift and stretch forth, thereby allowing him to carrying himself forward. The rider is actually at the apex of the post when the horse's other shoulder is already forward and that leg is on the ground bearing weight.

Now, we'll get a little more complicated, but in so doing, you will have a basic sense of what you're watching. Posting is done in conjunction with a horse's *diagonal*, another term you will hear frequently, mostly in phrases such as *right diagonal* and *wrong diagonal*. As your child is riding on a circle or a curved line, she is on her right diagonal when she is out of the saddle at the same time that the horse's outside shoulder is forward and the corresponding leg on the ground. At that same moment, the inside shoulder is unweighted and the corresponding leg is about to stretch forward, thus helping the horse to maintain his balance on a circle. Watch some other riders for a while, and you will start to see for yourself how posting and diagonals come into play.

perform in lesson after lesson and from riding them himself at times. And from experience, he is intuitive about children who are beginning to ride and what horses will be best for them.

Frequently, an instructor will put a small child on a pony because the animal's short stature and cute looks will be nonthreatening.

After all, if the object is to help the child enjoy herself so that she will want to ride again, what is the point of putting her on a large horse if there is a chance it could overwhelm her? Even the kindest one could frighten a small child simply because of his big stride and powerful feel.

However, size is not the only issue. A bigger child might feel perfectly secure on a large pony, a small horse, or even a medium-sized horse. The trick is to make the most successful match possible.

Even in cases where a pony would be the best choice, there are parents who take exception to the idea of their child riding one. ("A pony? I'm paying for *horse*back riding lessons!" I once heard a parent say.) To them a pony must seem inferior, a putdown to their child and perhaps to them. They will insist to an instructor that their child should be put on a horse, no matter what, even though they would never allow their small child to ride a bicycle that was too big!

So, what is the difference between ponies and horses? By the rules, only a measurement. Ponies can be no taller than 14 hands (a hand equals 4 inches) plus 2 inches, referred to as "fourteen two," or a total of 58 inches at the withers (the ridge between the shoulder bones). Horses cannot be shorter than that height. This is the only difference between ponies and horses. But of course each pony or horse is unique. Plenty of big horses are the best babysitters in the world, ones you could trust with your child's life. And there are ponies whom even advanced riders think twice about riding.

If you have confidence in your instructor, don't try to do his job. For sure, he has a better track record than you in matching up horse and rider! Soon enough your child will be gaining experience riding other horses, anyway. But for now, let her continue to ride the one who is giving her a good start.

A Small Investment in Equipment

Now that you have made the commitment to give your child riding lessons regularly, it is a good idea to invest in some riding apparel. Two items are important at this time: a hat and a pair of

Tack Shops to Get You Started

There are a myriad of catalog and online tack suppliers, with a full range of products for English and Western riders and their horses, some specializing in certain items. Here are a few generalists, good choices to furnish the couple of items you need right now.

Dover Saddlery
866-763-5517 or 800-406-8204
www.doversaddlery.com
Top-quality English tack, competitive prices.

State Line Tack
800-228-9208
www.statelinetack.com
English and Western name brands, good prices.

Chick's Discount Saddlery
800-444-2441
www.chicksaddlery.com
Discount prices, good online deals, English and Western.

eBay
www.ebay.com
Good source for used and new items. Search for "equestrian," "equestrian tack," or the name of the item you're looking for.

boots. Any tack shop should be able to provide suitable choices of both.

It there isn't a shop around, you can order from any of several popular catalog suppliers, taking care to provide proper measurements, as requested. Your instructor or the stable manager should be able to direct you to a shop or a catalog that they have used successfully. In addition, above is a list of tack suppliers, and many more options are listed in chapter 5.

While stables are usually happy to loan your child a riding helmet for a few lessons, they prefer riders to have their own hats after that. There is always the chance that the few hats they have will all be in use when your child arrives for her lesson. Unless she has her own or can borrow one from another child, she will be unable to ride at that time.

The hat you should buy is called a schooling helmet. Like protective headgear sold for other sports, it is intended as a piece of safety equipment, not wearing apparel. A variety of makes and models are available, all of which have a hard crown, a visor, and a chinstrap or harness. The hat should fit snugly enough so that it doesn't slip if your child takes a fall, and it should be worn *at all times* when she is riding. Don't try to make due with a bicycle helmet. True, it's protective headgear, but it protects against a different type of head injury.

The helmet you want will come in a range of prices, depending on whether it is covered in velveteen or velvet, and whether its

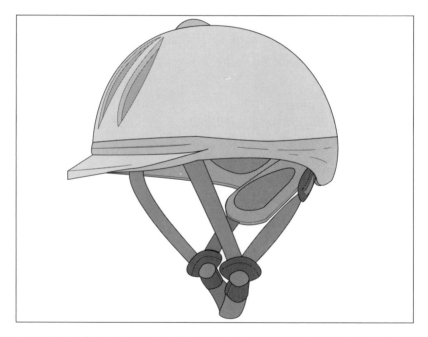

A good schooling helmet should have a hard crown, a visor, and a chinstrap or harness.

outer shell is made of fiberglass or other lightweight, impact-absorbing material. Be sure to choose one that carries an American Society of Testing Materials/Safety Equipment Institute (ASTM/SEI) seal of certification, which indicates that the helmet meets industry standards for protection and shock absorption. If you want to buy just one helmet for your child at this point, choose a hunt cap style that's nice enough looking that she can wear it in shows. Or, if you'd rather, buy a schooling helmet, and later you can buy a stretch velveteen cover to pull over it on show days. This doesn't look as smooth as a hunt cap, but it is an option.

The second item to purchase now is a pair of riding boots. Children usually wear paddock boots, which are ankle-high leather boots that lace up the front and have a hard toe and an oxford-style heel. Prices vary here, too. In the moderate range, the uppers will be of lower-quality leather and the sole will probably be of synthetic material or rubber, which is perfectly adequate. Some makers offer a choice of colors, too, including black, brown, and gray.

An alternative to paddock boots is high black riding boots. Children frequently wear an inexpensive black rubber version. On the plus side, these can survive the abuses of mud, dust, wetness, and other common stable conditions. However, many instructors dislike them because they often fit poorly through the calf area, and there is no "give" in the instep so that a rider can keep her heels down. Also, the toe is not reinforced to protect your child from a horse's misstep. Before you buy rubber boots, ask your instructor how he feels about them. If your budget can handle it, leather is a better choice, though it can be expensive, especially at the rate children grow! Look for sales and even check to see if anyone is selling a pair secondhand.

At this stage, slim-fitting jeans that will not ride up the leg work fine as riding pants. Of course, breeches are certainly an option, if you want to purchase them. They are made of stretchy fabric, usually a polyester/spandex mix, and they close tightly around the ankle with Velcro strips. Popular colors include rust, tan, brown, green, and navy.

Good paddock boots are ankle high, with laces or zippers, a reinforced toe, and a definite heel.

Not needed at this stage unless the weather is cold, but always a nice idea for a gift, would be a pair of riding gloves. When the temperature drops, regular knit gloves with leather palms and fingers are also workable. A riding crop is another option now.

No Coaching from the Sidelines, Please

Watching your child's lessons is fine, but not when your desire to help overwhelms you to the point that you begin calling out directions from the sidelines. This is a definite no and one that most instructors will nip in the bud politely but firmly the moment it starts. It is a marvel to them how quickly some parents think they are experts.

Of course, it seems innocent on your part. You are watching a lesson, and you can see your child having trouble doing something that looks easy to you. You are just certain that you can explain it better than the instructor, that your few well-chosen words can make the difference and help your child understand.

Well, think again. The instructor is trying to keep your child's attention, deal with her frustration, and get her past this difficult spot. Remember, riding is a completely new and complex experience, calling for the use of different muscles, coordinated in unfamiliar ways. From time to time there will be stumbling blocks, but calling to your child is just plain confusing. It breaks her concentration, because she must try to listen to both you and the instructor.

More than that, you can create a dangerous situation. Riding is complicated, and a rider has to pay attention to so many things: her own horse, her instructor, where she is going, and others around her. It is hard enough for youngsters to cope with all of these things at one time. And then your child hears your voice from outside the ring. Where is it coming from? She turns around to look. Now she is not looking where she is going, and she is not listening to the instructor, either, though she is still astride her horse. This is when an accident could easily happen.

Of course, it is frustrating to watch your child having a problem, and you are anxious to help her do better. But please, during the lesson, leave the teaching to the instructor. If you think you can help, explain it your way afterward. When your child is on the horse is not the right time. Be honest with yourself: If you feel you cannot stand silently by, it might be a good idea to go get a cup of coffee.

Learning to Communicate with Horses

One of the great pleasures of riding is learning how to work with the horse, making him understand what you want and to respond when you ask. It requires communicating in a common language, one you have both learned. It's not any different, really, than learning to communicate with your dog or cat. Except this time it's "horse talk" with its own vocabulary and responses.

In some ways, horses are no different from people. They can have good days and bad, act mellow or cranky, be full of vigor or stiff and ouchy, be brave or fearful. The better your child learns to "read" them, the more successful she will be in working with them. It doesn't happen overnight, but as she spends time around horses and rides more and more, she will become increasingly sensitive to them, learning how to react to them and get them to respond to her.

Horses are instinctive and have good memories, and they respond to a variety of signals from the rider's seat, hands, and legs working together but independently. Still, horses are a far cry from machines! They are living, breathing, reactive creatures, and the more a rider understands why and how a horse does what he does, the more willing and responsive the horse will be in following the rider's cues.

It is not uncommon to see a child who is on a horse for the first time, sitting on her mount in the middle of the ring, kicking away at the horse's sides to no avail. The horse just stands there, as if nothing is being asked of him, leading to comments from the rider along the lines of "This horse won't go. I don't like this horse. I want another one." Fortunately, such temper tantrums fall on deaf ears, and the instructor will likely quietly begin to explain that sitting properly and squeezing with the legs will produce a better result.

Three or four lessons later, such scenes are a thing of the past, as this same rider trots her horse around the ring. Did the horse improve? No, not this school horse. He already knows what to do. He was just waiting for his rider to learn how to communicate, to tell him in the proper way—in a manner of speaking, saying "please"—what it is she wanted him to do. And you know what? It worked. He complied.

Chapter Five

How to Survive in an Expensive Sport

By now your child has a new love in her life. Whether the name is Sonny, Jamsie, Patches, Sassy, Freckles, Al, or any one of countless other names, you are hearing it day in and day out. You are also buying an awful lot of carrots, and the grocery clerk is beginning to look a little puzzled.

Your child's face lights up when she talks about riding "her" horse, and you couldn't be happier. Except every once in a while, like when your neighbor said, "Riding? Oh, my goodness, that's so expensive. How can you possibly afford it?"

"Oh, dear," you think, "what have we started?"

To be sure, riding is a sport that *can* wind up costing a lot of money. There are always people, consciously or unconsciously, who will pressure you to spend more: other parents who buy their children fancy equipment, instructors who want their riders to go to more and bigger horse shows, or someone trying to interest you in buying a horse, long before you have even thought about the idea.

But this wonderful new experience for your child can be enjoyed at many different levels. Indeed, if you choose, expensive horses, trailers, and the finest equipment and apparel can be yours. However, riding can also be pursued at a far more modest level, and ultimately neither approach can appreciably add to or subtract from the pleasure of learning to ride. As when skiing, for example, you can wear a designer outfit or a much more moderately priced one. Either way, you will get the same enjoyment from a downhill run.

However, to be fair, riding is not different from any other sport in which your child might become involved, in which she would take regular lessons, and for which she would need to buy equipment. And it would be incorrect to pretend it is not a pricey sport, as well, involving expensive animals that need care, facilities that must be maintained, and other expenses. But riding can be a flexible sport, in which people of different economic means can partake. So don't be swayed by people who think riding will only wreck your budget. There is a niche for your child, and you can find it.

Keeping Lesson Costs in Check

Unless your youngster learns how to ride by getting up on that wonderful old pony on granddad's farm, when the question of horseback riding arises, it means, as you now know, you have to find a riding stable and sign up for lessons. And for a while, that's what costs money, pure and simple. The only equipment she's needed in this early period are a hat, which you probably bought within the first couple weeks, and riding shoes, which may actually be workable street shoes. This is not to say that she hasn't acquired some other things—tack shops and catalogs are very appealing—but they weren't "must buys." What *is* a must and a recurring expense is the cost of lessons. And, no surprise, it adds up!

The cost of lessons may not be a concern to you. Perhaps your child was taking some other kind of lesson, something she was getting tired of, and you've just switched the allotted money to the riding column. But if it is a concern or something that you're taking a hard look at now, before it becomes a problem, there are some possible options.

CHOOSING SEMIPRIVATE OR GROUP LESSONS

You already know about the three types of lessons. At any stable, they will be the same, in order of expense: Private lessons will be the most expensive, semiprivate lessons a little less so, and group lessons the least expensive.

Initially, you're not going to have a lot of room to maneuver. The trainer likely insisted on your child's first lesson being private. A few more private lessons might be a good idea, unless the instructor is absolutely sure that your youngster can handle herself on a horse. Dollars spent at this point help to build a safe beginning for your child's riding experience, and pinching pennies now is simply unwise. But after that, semiprivate lessons, if you want to trim the costs just a little, or group lessons, if you want to save more, are definitely to be considered.

By all means, have a talk with the instructor and be forthright about your concerns. As the costs mount up, no one wants to make riding a gut-wrenching experience for you. That is no fun at all, and your anxiety will transmit to your child.

What can your instructor suggest? Certainly, a lesson a week provides continuity and a good pace for learning. But would he be opposed to a lesson every ten days or two weeks? What about a private lesson every other week? You need to explore the possibilities.

As discussed before, no one will dispute the value of private lessons as a learning tool. Working one-on-one with someone will always mean quicker progress. After all, if a rider is having difficulty with something, the instructor can devote all his time—the rest of the lesson, if necessary—to helping the child correct a particular stumbling block. No other type of lesson allows quite this kind of attention.

Nevertheless, the trade-offs and positive gains from semiprivate and group lessons are clear. Because in dividing his attention among two or more riders, and commenting in turn on what they are doing correctly and incorrectly, the instructor introduces the value of competition. Kept friendly, competition encourages youngsters to be as good as one another, or better, and can be productive. No one wants to get left behind, stuck at the walk when everyone else is trotting, or, worse yet, stopped dead in her tracks and unable to move the horse forward at all. Children have fun in semiprivate and group lessons. They show off, compete, and encourage and help each other. And riding in a group lesson will be her first taste of riding and maneuvering in traffic, something she will have to do if she ever decides to enter a horse show.

The downside of semiprivate and group lessons is the matter of scheduling. You must deal with someone else's schedule, that of another child and parent, if you want to set up a semiprivate lesson. Or, in the case of a group, your child may be joining one that is already in existence. But stables are aware of their clients' overall schedules. If there are lots of children in a class, lessons will be set up after school and on weekends, so working something out is far from insurmountable.

You may also wonder about changing stables, if you can find another in your area where lesson prices are lower. But be careful. As with most other things, you get what you pay for, whether it's the caliber of the instruction, the horses, or the facility. You chose the stable you and your child are at because you liked all those things, so before you switch, see if you can't work things out where you are. Good riding instructors, like any good teacher, want kids to learn how to ride. If they see that you and your child are intent on riding, they'll work with you as best they can to create a workable lesson plan. Depending on your budget, you can make private lessons a sometime thing used for extra help here and there when your child hits a stumbling block or a plateau, or there's something she just wants extra help with.

OFFSETTING LESSON COSTS

Perhaps because they recognize how hard it is to become a good rider and they remember how long it took to gain their own proficiency, stable personnel are impressed with dedicated young riders. Most of them will try to help a youngster who needs to offset some of her expenses, if they possibly can.

If your child shows interest and commitment, after a few lessons it doesn't hurt to inquire if such assistance is ever an option. When available, most likely it will involve doing some form of barn work. This can include everyday chores like cleaning or mucking out stalls, giving the horses their grain and hay, scrubbing and filling water buckets, and sweeping up. Some barns operate on an exchange program and trade chores for lessons, while others have paid help, but the latter still need people to cover chores on paid workers' days off. Also, there are often odd jobs to do, like painting fences and jumps, pulling (shortening) manes, and cleaning boarders' and school tack (saddles and bridles).

Of course, as simple as many stable chores sound, you and your youngster should get used to barn life before you commit to any chores. Barn work is heavy labor, it is time-consuming, and the "pay" is low; that is, your child will do a fair amount of work for every lesson she gets. You will have to commit to driving your child to the stable extra times each week or for longer stays at lesson time. And you may wind up driving her to the stable at seven o'clock on Saturday and Sunday mornings, if one of her chores is weekend feeding.

There is also a limit to how much work a very young or very small child can do. To her, it doesn't seem like "work," and even the smallest child seems to muck a stall and do other chores quite well. Some children are so motivated that they would happily live at the stable, and it remains for the parents to call a halt so that schoolwork and other responsibilities are not forgotten.

Parents, too, may be able to help offset lesson costs by trading skills and expertise, as well as even goods and services for a rate cut on some lessons. Maybe making an arrangement will reduce the price on a series of lessons, or maybe you and the stable's management can work out something that will mean a reduced rate for your child's lessons for longer than that.

Put your thinking cap on. Any number of things could need doing. For instance, depending on your abilities, inclination, and contacts (professional and otherwise), the possibilities might include painting the barn, hauling manure away, trucking in sand for a riding ring, repairing stalls and anything else that needs attention, putting on a new roof, supplying lumber and other goods for various projects, bookkeeping, helping at a local horse show, designing and printing a promotional brochure for the stable or a prize list for an upcoming show, or donating equipment the stable needs. Look around: The needs may be obvious, or maybe you'll see something management has thought about and now you can make an offer.

Finding Equipment to Fit Your Budget

One day when there are several riders in the ring, stop and watch for a minute. Who is your eye drawn to? Chances are, it is the best rider, the one who seems to be most "at one" with her horse, asking for and receiving responses in the most polished and effortless manner.

It doesn't matter whether that rider is outfitted in the finest attire, right down to her custom-made black leather boots or butter-soft suede chaps. First you are drawn to her horsemanship and the partnership in motion that she and her horse are creating. What she's wearing, the saddle she's sitting in, and the bridle her horse is wearing are part of the picture certainly, but they're not what you're drawn to. Nor will you notice if that same excellent rider is dressed in clothes that are not top of the line.

To borrow a phrase, "clothes do not make the rider." Riding does. Your eye is drawn to horsemanship, not to the accessories of the sport. And indeed, if a rider and her horse are performing poorly, all the embellishments in the world won't help the picture. Happily, there is a price range for virtually everything you need in this sport, from schooling helmets to breeches, bridles to horse blankets, saddles to nutritional supplements, and all things in between.

Even if you don't need most of what's available at this point, it's a good time to check out some of the many vendors supplying the horse industry and identify some in your price range. The sidebar on pages 58–61 gives a good basic selection, but you'll be amazed at the hundreds upon hundreds of suppliers in existence, now at your fingertips from any Web search. Chances are you'll enjoy uncovering your own finds, beyond those listed here. Part of the fun of being at a barn is sharing knowledge with the others. And good for you when the new kids on the block find a source that others may not know about!

Making Shows Affordable

There's no hiding the fact that from the time you start going to the stable, you'll be hearing about horse shows. It may just drift in one ear and out the other, or you may find yourself talking to parents of other beginning riders about what may be in store for you and your child.

Like everything else in this sport, price looms large, and it's not unreasonable for you to be wondering, as your very first question, what's this going to cost? Horseback riding is such a huge sport, with so many disciplines and breeds competing at shows, so many organizations sanctioning their own shows, plus local stables and other groups holding shows, that there is no clear answer or even reasonable sliding scale as to what going to a show will cost.

However, in no way does this mean that you must remain in the dark. Look to chapter 9 for an in-depth discussion, but here are some ideas to get you started.

First, before that first show presents itself as a possibility, question your child's instructor about showing and what it will cost. Look for concrete answers. At this early point in your child's riding, you really have no say in what it will cost, other than yes or no to the whole idea. So it is best to become informed beforehand.

Ask your instructor: What will the entry fees at a small, local schooling show be, and, on average, how many classes will a beginning rider enter? What will it cost to rent the school horse your child will ride, and what will it cost to van him to the show? What will the instructor's training fee at the show be? What will it cost to braid the mane, and are there any other expenses? The other major expense will be show clothes for your child, but that is under your control.

Tack Suppliers

These are all reputable vendors, most of whom have been in the business for years. They'll stand behind their products, and for someone new to the sport, they provide a good place to start for whatever you need. Some, including Dover Saddlery, State Line Tack, and Chick's Discount Saddlery, have large, general inventories and are good places to look for those first items. Others are best known in certain categories. Most have catalogs, and all can be reached online. The selection in children's sizes varies from dealer to dealer, but overall there's plenty to choose from.

English Tack
The Bridle Path & Clothing Co.
www.thebridlepath.com
877-658-4277
English tack.

Dominion Saddlery
800-282-2587
www.saddlery.com
Quality English apparel and tack.

Dover Saddlery
866-763-5517 or 800-406-8204
www.doversaddlery.com
Top-quality English apparel and tack, competitive prices. Catalog coupons and sales. Stores in Wellesley, Massachusetts, and Hockessin, Delaware, with a bargain basement at the Massachusetts store.

Wild Horse Feathers
800-298-4998
www.wildhorsefeathers.com
Apparel, gifts, and Breyer horses. Very child oriented, though adult sizes are available, too.

Western Tack

Denny Sergeant's Western World
800-383-3669
www.sergeantswestern.com
Range of tack and clothing. Has its own custom line.

Hobby Horse
800-569-5885
www.hobbyhorseinc.com
Beautiful Western apparel. Good selection in girls', youth, and plus sizes.

Horse Saddle Shop
866-880-2121
www.horsesaddleshop.com
Western saddles.

Smith Brothers
800-784-5449 or 866-763-5480
www.smithbrothers.com
Long-time supplier, offers coupons.

English and Western Tack

Affordable Saddles & Tack
888-726-3906
www.affordable-tack.com
English and Western saddles and bridles.

Big Dee's Tack & Vet Supply
800-321-2142
www.bigdweb.com
Mostly supplies and tack, both English and Western; some riding apparel.

Chick's Discount Saddlery
800-444-2441
www.chicksaddlery.com
Good discount source, especially for basics. Weekly online specials. Store in Harrington, Delaware.

Jeffers Equine
800-JEFFERS
www.jeffersequine.com
Good prices, big selection. Especially useful for supplements and barn supplies. Western tack, some English.

SaddleOnline.com
www.saddleonline.com
800-967-2335
English and Western saddles.

State Line Tack
800-228-9208
www.statelinetack.com
Name brands at reduced prices.

SuitAbility
800-207-0256
www.suitability.com
Sewing patterns for riding apparel and horse equipment; children's and other sizes.

Stable Supplies

American Livestock Supply, Inc.
800-356-0700
www.americanlivestock.com
Supplements, barn supplies and equipment, some tack (both English and Western), and blankets.

BMB
800-8HALTER
www.bmbtack.com
Horse clothing and Western tack.

Chariton Vet Supply
800-748-7837
www.charitonvet.com
Good prices on supplements.

Farnam Horse
800-234-2269
www.farnamhorse.com
Supplements, grooming products, and stable supplies.

United Vet Equine
800-328-6652
www.unitedvetequine.com
Good source for grooming supplies, supplements, and wormers.

Valley Vet Supply
800-356-1005
www.valleyvet.com
Supplements and stable supplies.

Used Tack

eBay
www.ebay.com
Search for "equestrian," "equestrian tack," "saddles," and more. English and Western. Used and new items. Great prices if you find what you want, but make sure shipping costs are fair.

Local Options

In your local area, look for the following:

- Used tack sales and consignments at tack shops.

- Tack swap nights organized by area horseman's association or other organization (or put one together yourself).

- Tack-for-sale notices (used items or new) on bulletin boards at local stables (yours and others), feed stores, and tack shops.

- Classified ads in local horseman's newspapers, delivered free to feed stores and tack shops. Also, classifieds in local general-circulation newspapers.

Besides asking about show expenses, keep these points in mind: (1) Start slowly. Go to one show, then decide on another. This way, you won't start feeling pressured. You'll have a much clearer idea about expenses, as well as how much your child is really enjoying it. (2) Show locally, if at all possible, at a small schooling show held at your own stable. This will keep the cost of vanning your horse to the show moderate, and if you're on home turf, nonexistent. (3) Unless you're adverse to them, consider buying used riding clothes, at least for now. Especially if your child is growing fast, and until you've decided if showing is really for you, it makes good sense.

To Buy or Not to Buy a Horse?

The short answer is not to buy, at least not for a good long while. You'll be amazed at how people will start to put the bug in your ear or before too long will have a "great deal" on a horse that you should consider.

Chapters 11 and 12 say much more on the subject, in case in the future horse owning does become a point of discussion. But for now, you need to keep in mind just a couple things.

First, buying a horse is only the start of what this venture will cost you. Or, as horse people like to say, "It's not the purchase price; it's the upkeep." To whatever extent you think riding is (or isn't) expensive, you haven't seen anything until you own a horse! This is not to say that for most people who own, or have owned horses, it doesn't count as one of the most rewarding experiences of their lives. It is that, without a doubt. But it doesn't come cheap.

Yes, there are many ways to manage the budget when it comes to horse-keeping expenses, too. But it's a far cry from finding a great price on a schooling helmet. You will now own a large animal who needs food and housing, blankets, and other supplies. He must also be watched over carefully, exercised, trained, and shod, and he needs health care. Loving him, which you will do with abandon, is the only thing that comes free!

The other thing to remember is that there are no "deals" in buying a horse. You get what you pay for. Especially as a newcomer to the sport, beware of unscrupulous people who have an "unbelievable bargain" for you. "Yes," the seller will agree, "it's a bit early, but you really shouldn't let this one go." Well, you certainly should. Particular types of horses of a given age range, training, ability, and so forth sell within a particular price range in different geographic regions. People know what their horses are worth, and any deviation from accepted parameters calls for close examination, if you even consider such an offer at all.

When the time is right, if that is the route you decide to take, educate yourself and shop wisely. You and your trainer should make up a shopping list of what you want in a horse versus what you want to pay. Then, with this professional by your side, you can start looking. But please, not before.

Keeping the Reins in *Your* Hands

Your child is learning to ride a horse, hopefully with enough skill to truly enjoy the sport, safely and securely, in whatever ways appeal to her. It is worth repeating: It can be done with a great deal of money, or it can be done modestly. The kind of lessons your child takes and the frequency with which she takes them, the equipment you buy for her, and the amount and type of showing you do (if any) are all adjustable areas. And because you have chosen to bring your child to a stable that, from the beginning, felt comfortable to you, it is probable that there are like-minded parents there with whom to compare notes. Almost everyone is willing to share ideas and solutions for making their way successfully in this sport.

So don't be afraid to keep the reins in *your* hands. Enjoy the sport as you can afford it. Even on a budget, your child can wind up being one of the best riders at the stable.

Chapter Six

Walk, Trot, . . . and Now Canter

*T*he lessons have been going along well, and your child is starting to look quite comfortable on a horse. From that first day when the instructor was always right at her side, holding the horse on a lead line, your child advanced to riding in a circle, the horse still attached to a line and still controlled by the instructor. Next, she began riding on her own, the horse responding only to what your child told him to do.

Your child learned to make the horse walk forward from a stand, and stop again. Then she learned to steer him right and left and to get him to trot. Then one exciting day your child finally got the knack of posting—on the correct diagonal, too. And confidently, she trotted around the ring, first one way and then the other.

Now, another red-letter day: Your child has just cantered her horse for the first time. This is definitely a milestone! Know one thing about school horses: While they are kind and patient, they are also sticklers for doing something correctly. No doubt you watched your youngster struggle at first, her legs saying "go" while, without meaning to, her hands and upper body said "stop." The horse waited until she put it all together. Then off they went, she with a look of amazement and excitement on her face. She is really riding, and she knows it.

What a different feeling! Even though the trot seemed like a lot of movement after the walk, the canter is a big, bold, ground-covering gait compared to the trot. The horse's body is truly moving now. Where his back was essentially horizontal at the walk and trot, it is now tilting like a seesaw. Three cheers for your young rider!

What You're Both Learning Now

Riding is getting to be more and more fun. Now that your child has graduated to the canter, even though she has trouble with it sometimes, she feels like one of the group. After all, the canter is difficult, and everyone fumbles, but that's okay. When she takes a group lesson, she will feel as though she can keep up.

Her trot is getting more secure and steadier, too. When the instructor asks the group to trot around the ring together, your child does a pretty good job of staying on the rail and keeping the proper distance behind the horse ahead of her. By now, she may have also tried riding another horse or two. True, she may have become very attached to the one she started with, but it is good for a rider to test her abilities and see how other horses feel. When presented the right way, trying new horses feels like a step up, too.

And, oh, the vocabulary! Sometimes, how you wished you had a dictionary (before you had the glossary at the end of this book, of course!). Like yesterday, when your youngster talked all the way home about how Freckles just wouldn't take his right lead. The instructor kept telling her to sit back, but she just couldn't get it. Then they went back to the trot, changed reins across the half school, and when your child asked for the left lead canter, she got it right away. "But at least," she finished, "we ended on a good note, and my instructor says that is very important. Because then the horse won't get into a bad habit."

"Of course, dear," you say, feeling a little helpless. Leads, changing reins, half schools, good notes—you had no idea there was such a language. Well, take heart. It is really not that complicated. As other parents will tell you, in short order you will know enough to make the proper response. And soon enough, you will really be showing your stuff, saying to your child something like, "So, how did your transitions go today? Were you able to drive him up into that right lead canter okay?" Yes, indeed, it will happen.

Getting a Little Nervous?

Okay, admit it. There are days when this still makes you a little nervous. You were fine when your child was walking and stopping the horse, over and over. And when she began trotting, it was okay, too. Granted, she got jounced around a little and a couple of times looked like she was going to slip off. But she stayed on and, in fact, the horse she was riding didn't look like he was going anywhere in a hurry, either.

However, the canter is something else! As far as you are concerned, that is *fast*. Well, maybe not fast, but it looks a whole lot different from what your youngster was doing before.

Then there was that one day, when they were all in the ring having their lesson. Another youngster wasn't paying attention and let her horse plow right into the horse ahead of her. Nothing actually happened, but the horse who got bumped pinned his ears flat back and looked pretty annoyed.

And now that you are thinking about it, there was that other rider, the one who got thrown from her horse. Well, you guess she wasn't really thrown. Actually, it did look like she sort of slid off. And she got back on in a flash, as if she didn't want anyone to even notice. Except you did—you saw it all!

But are you noticing something else while you are having your anxiety attacks? Your child is smiling. She seems to be having the time of her young life.

TAKING THE SPILLS WITH THE THRILLS

There is an old adage that seven falls makes a rider, twelve falls a horseman. Yes, sooner or later, your child will fall off her horse. And most times, only her pride will get hurt—and hopefully not even that.

Usually, it is just a fall. A combination slide and tumble after she loses her balance, perhaps tries vainly to regain it, and then reaches the point of no return. It can take on the look of a slow-motion video, or your child can wind up on the ground so fast she hardly knows what happened.

Maybe your child just wasn't balanced as well as she might have been, and stride by stride, the horse's motion just kept unseating her more and more. Or she forgot to steer, and when the horse swerved one way, your child went the other. Or the horse was startled or just feeling good and gave a buck when least expected. Suffice it to say, there could be any number of reasons that end the same way—in a simple mishap.

As long as she is not really hurt, the important thing is for your child to get on her feet and back on the horse as quickly as she can. The instructor will encourage this because mentally it pushes your child past the accident. Getting back on the horse establishes that the rider is in charge again and helps to quickly restore her confidence.

When your child fell off, the instructor and other riders probably shouted, "Hooray, now we get a chocolate cake!" It is a tradition at lots of stables for riders who've fallen to bring a baked goodie to their next lesson to help make light of the episode. At some places, chocolate is a must; elsewhere the treat just has to be sweet and delicious. But it's a fun custom that often goes beyond just *children* falling off, I can tell you! There was a period when I kept several yummy recipes handy. While no one wants to see you take a spill, it does mean goodies for all at your next lesson.

And what should you do when your youngster falls off? In a word, *relax*. And take a breath. This is really no different from tumbling off a bicycle, falling at an ice skating rink, or stumbling when running after a ball. If you react badly, even if your child is shaken up, or a little bumped and bruised, it will only get her more upset.

You knew it was going to happen one of these days, and as anyone who rides will tell you, falling off is no big deal. It's best for you to stay cool, give her a hug later on, and chuckle about it. Then get out the electric mixer and your favorite recipe. This might be her first cake, but it probably won't be her last!

OVERCOMING FEARS AND PREPARING FOR FALLS

It would be unrealistic to think that at some time your child won't be frightened by a riding incident. It could be because of a fall she takes or sees a friend take, or it could be caused by a horse who gets balky and refuses to do what he is asked, maybe even becoming tense or jumpy. If anything makes your child fearful, encourage her to talk about it. It will probably be something that you and her instructor can help to dispel.

Particularly with a beginning rider, who has yet to build up time in the saddle and positive experiences, fear can quickly stall progress and actually erode what progress has been made. The horse, a very sensitive animal, picks up on the rider's fear and begins to exhibit his own fearful traits. Breaking the cycle may require taking a youngster back to a point in her training where she feels completely confident and then moving forward again.

Overall, the more knowledge and the better the skills, the less likely that a negative event will have any lasting effects. Because one of the basic fears of a young and inexperienced rider is falling and getting hurt, teaching her to fall properly can be very valuable. Ask the instructor to discuss this with the riders and, if possible, to teach them how to do a vaulting dismount at the walk, trot, and even the canter.

You can help, too, by discussing how to fall with your child, so that key points will stay in her mind. First, when the rider feels herself coming off the horse and knows she is past the point of reversing it, she should make a conscious effort to relax and think "limp." Exhaling the breath relaxes muscles, as opposed to the common reaction of holding the breath, which stiffens the body and can result in pulled muscles and broken bones.

When falling off a horse headfirst, which is quite common, it's important to tuck the chin and shield the head with raised arms, bent at the elbows. Finally, the rider should roll when landing, and the momentum from this will probably bring the rider right-side up, to about the same position she was originally in on the horse. At this point, most likely all she'll need is a brushing off.

You should rehearse these points from time to time with your child. Practicing tumbling or gymnastics, which she may be able to take at school, is also helpful. When the real falls come, the preparation will pay off.

Equipment Considerations at This Point

As long as you have purchased a schooling helmet and a pair of paddock boots, or other sturdy, ankle-high, lace-up shoes, with a heel and hard toe, you are set for now. Until your child gets close to going to her first horse show, nothing else is an absolute necessity.

EQUIPMENT TO CONSIDER

Beyond a schooling helmet and boots, depending on the time of year, you may want to purchase a few other items for your child at this stage of the game.

Particularly if she is planning to ride through the winter, investing in a pair of warmer boots is something to think about. You can buy fleece-lined paddock boots or try a pair of those tan-colored woodsman's boots, with the cold-weather lining and padded ankle collar. They work fine, too, as long as the rubber sole has narrow ridges rather than wide, deep cleats.

Leather riding gloves can keep hands warm, especially if they are lined or if ski-glove liners are worn underneath. If it's summer, a pair of gloves is still a good idea, as wearing them makes it easier to grip reins that can get slippery from sweaty hands.

Breeches are still an option. The long-legged look is certainly very attractive as your child's riding improves, but for now, breeches are still in the optional category. However, a lot depends on the formality or informality of your stable. If all the other children are riding in breeches, chances are your child is going to want a pair, too.

The same can be said for chaps. Ask your instructor's opinion before you buy them, however. Some instructors don't like them, particularly for beginning riders, because they think that they give a false sense of security. The leather provides a little extra grip, and when the rider switches to boots and breeches, as she will if she wants to show, she may find that her legs slide around more than she is used to. But do ask; some instructors are more tolerant of chaps than others. Plus, they do save wear and tear on pant legs. You can, by the way, get quite a good fit with off-the-rack chaps. Even if custom-made chaps are ultimately in your future, your child is still growing, so why not leave them there, for the time being at least?

EQUIPMENT YOU STILL DON'T NEED

Buying the equipment your child needs and dealing with her wants that are based on seeing what other children have can be two very different matters. Only you can determine how well you will survive the pressure to buy expensive or fancy equipment. Even if you can't match all the new things another youngster gets (and who says you even want to, anyway?), a small purchase now and then—maybe a reward when your child has an especially good lesson—will still surely be appreciated.

By now, you two have undoubtedly spent time poking around your local tack shop and combing through some tempting riding catalogs and Web sites. Like those for any other sport or hobby, riding catalogs and Web sites have a vast and wonderfully appealing array of equipment, clothing, and whatnot to persuade even the most disciplined buyer. Of course, you will succumb now and then—believe me, everyone does! This, too, is part of the fun of the sport. Your child is now one of those "horsey people" and, one thing's for sure: You will never be at a loss for gift ideas and special treats!

Some items can be bought too soon, however, no matter how convincing your youngster sounds. One is a saddle, which is a major expenditure even for a moderately priced model. In time, it will be a very appropriate purchase, because an advancing rider will start to appreciate a saddle that is broken in to conform to her own body. However, for a beginning rider, who is still working to develop her basic, overall skills and is not yet sensitive to the feel of a saddle, the stable's school tack is fine.

Many children are also very attracted to spurs and cannot wait to wear them. Advanced riders frequently use them, and the look of boots and spurs must appear very dashing to a youngster. But used carelessly and excessively by an unskilled rider, spurs can cause the horse to bolt or otherwise "blow up" and possibly land the rider on the ground. Wait for the instructor to ask you to buy spurs and be sure that he feels confident that your child is ready to use them. It likely won't be for quite some time.

Keeping It Fun

Your child is having fun. She is making steady progress and is undoubtedly very pleased with herself. And so are you. It is exciting to watch her tackle something new, stay with it, and begin to develop some proficiency.

Careful, though: Don't be overly enthusiastic. Encouragement, in the right amount, can keep her going, but in excess it can have the opposite effect. On those days when things just didn't go well, and your child is down in the dumps wondering if she will ever be a good rider, a few understanding words like "You'll catch on, you'll see" can mean the difference between trying a little harder the next time and giving up.

But pushing too hard, always prodding your child to new accomplishments and new goals beyond her comprehension, can backfire. If you keep telling her she is good but could be better, she may stop hearing the first part. While you mean to build her confidence, you actually could be eroding it. If she stops being pleased with herself, her pleasure in riding may end altogether.

Of course, you know best how much to push your child. But telling a youngster who has just learned to canter that in five years the whole family expects to watch her at the regional finals is laying on too much pressure.

So, make sure it stays fun. As any rider will tell you, it is too difficult a sport to master if the fun disappears.

Being an Interested, Knowledgeable Parent

As your child becomes more involved with riding, hopefully you, too, will feel more comfortable around the stable. Stable people, you will find, love to talk about their horses and will be happy to answer your questions. Besides watching your child ride, there are other things to catch your attention. And there's plenty to read on all phases of the sport in horse magazines and in your local tack shop's selection of books.

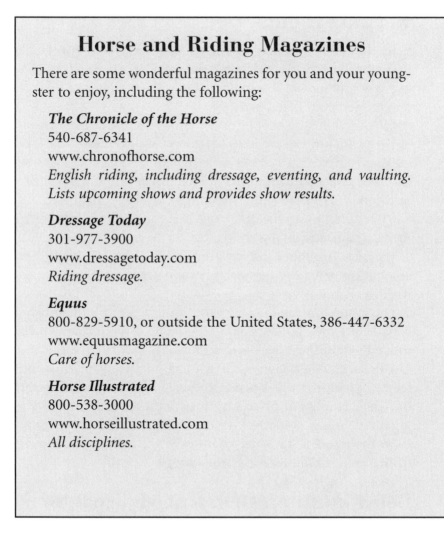

Horse and Riding Magazines

There are some wonderful magazines for you and your youngster to enjoy, including the following:

The Chronicle of the Horse
540-687-6341
www.chronofhorse.com
English riding, including dressage, eventing, and vaulting. Lists upcoming shows and provides show results.

Dressage Today
301-977-3900
www.dressagetoday.com
Riding dressage.

Equus
800-829-5910, or outside the United States, 386-447-6332
www.equusmagazine.com
Care of horses.

Horse Illustrated
800-538-3000
www.horseillustrated.com
All disciplines.

It's no secret that with horseback riding, as with anything else, the more you know, the more you can appreciate. Then you will really understand how well your child is doing.

Horse & Rider
877-717-8928 in the United States and Canada; elsewhere, 386-447-6306
www.horseandrider.com
Western riding, horse care, and training.

Practical Horseman
877-717-8929
www.practicalhorsemanmag.com
English riding.

Western Horseman
800-877-5278
www.westernhorseman.com
Everything Western.

Young Rider
800-365-4421
www.youngrider.com
All disciplines, with a focus on youngsters.

Tack shops often carry the current issues of these magazines, as do major bookstore chains. Or you can order single issues (often on a free trial basis) from the publisher. Try them out, one by one, and see what you like. Then, just maybe, one of the magazines will start arriving at your home, a gift for your beginning rider. How's that for an idea?

Chapter Seven

Starting to Jump

A jumping horse draws attention. Whether he is cantering down to a single fence or negotiating a complicated course of elaborate, colorful obstacles, the picture of this powerful animal launching himself into the air time and again turns heads. The idea that horses can thrust themselves up with such ease and agility, clear the hurdle with legs tucked, descend gracefully, balance themselves, and move on to the next fence is exciting to contemplate. And the feeling, when you are in the saddle, is even more exciting.

It is the rare child whose eyes aren't riveted on a rider jumping a horse. The more assertive announce, even as they are taking their first lessons, that they, too, are going to do that. Though others may not be so bold initially, as their confidence grows, you can sense their increased interest as they watch a jumper perform. In fact, among more timid riders, it undoubtedly says something about a child's growing self-confidence when she says, "Do you think I could try that sometime?"

And why not? When you see a group of children, one after another, jumping fences in a lesson, their enjoyment is absolutely infectious. With the proper guidance and prior training, youngsters pop over small fences with obvious relish and delight in their accomplishments. Some are excited to be doing the very littlest jumps, hardly more than a bouncy step for even the smallest horse or pony. Others are eager to keep advancing as soon as they show they are ready. All in all, children's jumping lessons

Western Riders Don't Jump

Well, Western riders don't jump courses of fences, anyway. But Western horses must be able to jump single obstacles on the trail, when asked, as well as in the show ring, either with their rider up or leading their horse over a jump from the ground. And it's something the Western horse must do with just as much willingness and skill as English hunters or jumpers.

But Western-riding youngsters are working on many different activities, as well. Ask what challenges lie ahead for them, and they will likely talk about reining, cutting, barrel racing (for girls) and other rodeo events, and perfecting the exacting and intriguing moves required in various show classes—among them backing and side passes; crossing a bridge; opening, going through, and closing a gate; jumping a log; and hauling a bag of rattling garbage.

Choosing American Quarter Horses most often, with Paints, Appaloosas, Arabians, and Morgans as other favored breeds, Western riders train their mounts to the smooth movements needed for a long day in the saddle: the gentle, slow jog and easy, rocking-chair lope. In attitude and approach, the activities and events popular with America's "working horses of the West" and their riders reflect a colorful history and lore.

are fun times, filled with giggles and laughter, oohs and ahhs, whoops and hollers. With few exceptions, youngsters love it.

Most horses do, too, or so it seems. Some do it better than others because they are more athletic or better trained, but almost all horses have some natural aptitude for jumping. If your stable caters to English hunt seat riders, among the school horses there will be some steady, dependable jumpers who will safely take your child over her first small hurdles.

Indeed, her first jump, a tiny crossrail made by two poles forming a wide, squat X, will be a new milestone in riding. Introduced at just the right moment, under the instructor's watchful eye—though with a seemingly casual, low-key air—it will give your child another reason to feel very proud of herself.

Is Your Child Ready to Jump?

Of course, you've seen it coming. Your child is more and more confident about her riding. She has watched other youngsters jumping their horses and having fun doing it. And lately, she has begun talking about jumping and wondering when her instructor will let her start, as if it is the natural next step in her riding education. As long as *she* wants to learn how, she is absolutely right. When the instructor also feels that she has advanced sufficiently in her training, particularly that she is balanced and secure on her horse, she will be allowed to start jumping.

Make no mistake: There will be plenty of snags and stumbling blocks along the road to learning how to jump, just as there are to all other aspects of riding. After all, it is a complex sport to master, and jumping is certainly a challenging part of it. Therefore, just as you made sure your child really wanted to learn how to ride in the first place—and wasn't being pushed into it—so you must be sure that she is the one who wants to learn to jump.

A child will most likely let her instructor know when she feels ready, and most are usually very direct about it. "When will I be able to jump? I'd like to try that" is a common statement from a young rider at some point. It indicates her confidence in her riding ability, a feeling that the horse, too, will feel. Couple that mental readiness with a solid foundation of riding skills on the flat, and jumping becomes an easy, exciting next step in your child's riding experience.

Is It Too Soon to Jump?

Most youngsters want to jump, no doubt about it. True, they love all types of riding, but practicing the walk, trot, and canter lesson after lesson isn't as much fun as it was a while ago—at least, not when your child sees other kids at the barn jumping their horses.

But sometimes the scenario can present problems. Privately, her instructor may feel your child is not quite ready. Her trot work is coming along nicely, but her cantering is still shaky. She can't sit securely yet, and as the horse keeps going, she tends to get pulled forward, out of the saddle. As long as the horse trots into the crossrail quietly, takes a small, relaxed jump, and trots out just as quietly, it will be fine. But if the horse jumps a little too big and canters off, your child could be in trouble.

She is wearing the instructor down, though, with her pleading, so he decides to let her try. Anyway, he reasons, it will make her realize how important flat work is. Unfortunately, jumping before she is ready can also scare your child.

Then again, maybe she's riding with a group of more advanced beginners, the rest of whom are truly ready to start over fences. The instructor is aware that your child's flat work isn't as secure as theirs. And if she hasn't brought up the subject of jumping yet herself, you can probably assume that she doesn't feel ready yet. She may even let slip a meek "Do I have to?" as an indicator that she's just not ready to start jumping.

If the rest of the class is ready, it would be much easier if the instructor could just push her along a little. The problem is, if she tries jumping before she's ready, her body language will telegraph exactly that, and the horse, sensing it, may refuse to take the jump, a scenario that can unsettle your child even more.

Hopefully, the instructor will get to know your child well enough that he will not try to push her into something that makes her uncomfortable at this early stage. The other class members can continue to jump, while your child waits in the center of the ring, clear of the fences. She may be a little embarrassed at being singled out in front of her friends, but that will fade soon enough. Better that than a fall and possibly setting up a fearful situation that later will have to be undone.

You and the instructor can work out a remedy. Perhaps there is another beginner group, not quite as advanced as the one she is in, where everyone will be ready to jump at about the same time. Or you might be able to arrange for a few private lessons to give your child the extra help she needs. It may only take a few weeks to bring about the necessary improvement and give her confidence, but just this short delay in starting her over fences can mean the difference between creating an early problem and beginning on a positive note.

Starting Slowly

When your child definitely seems ready to start jumping, you can't help but begin worrying again: The flat work has been going so well, and having the horse keep his four feet on the ground seems a little safer than letting him carry your youngster over jumps. Must we change that, you wonder? Well, hold on a minute, before you send only anxious feelings her way.

Starting a beginning rider over jumps is a very scaled-down version of some of the other jumping you have probably seen at the stable. Erase the image of a rider cantering down to a three-foot fence, turning left three strides after it, coming back up over two fences on a diagonal line, then turning right and jumping still another fence, and another, and another. Those performances are a long way beyond anything your child will be doing now.

Initially, your child won't actually be jumping at all, but simply trotting over wood poles placed on the ground. They are called ground poles or trotting poles, and they are 8 to 12 feet long and usually painted white or left their natural color. This careful beginning is totally within her scope and ability, as she continues to ride those wonderful school horses who have gone this route a thousand times before. Despite her best efforts to maintain her jumping position, if she becomes a little loose and wobbly, if she lurches left or right, falls forward or jerks back, swings her legs or yanks on the horse's mouth, her mount will be as forgiving and accepting as any horse can be. And when need be, he especially won't mind this beginning rider grabbing a clump of mane and hanging on.

By repeatedly trotting over single poles on the ground, and then the very lowest, nonthreatening jumps, your child will secure her jumping position and gain confidence in this new phase of riding. With a slow, deliberate start and many steps in between, well into the future she may indeed be jumping three-foot courses with all the skill and confidence she needs.

Safe Jumping

As with any educational endeavor, your child's progress in riding is guided by a simple principle: Each step forward builds on what has gone before. She proved her ability at the walk before she could trot, and similarly at the trot before she could canter.

As she begins jumping, you will understand why the instructor insists repeatedly that good flat work is the basis of everything that comes after. Your youngster has to be balanced and secure in the saddle at the walk, trot, and canter, and she has to be able to use her arms, legs, and seat independently of each other.

Each part of the body has to perform prescribed functions without interfering with what the rest of the body is doing. For instance, in stopping or slowing a horse's pace, the rider must be able to pull back on the reins while sitting deep in the saddle, rather than being pulled out of it. When asking for the canter, your child must be able to bring just her lower outside leg back (the one closest to the outside rail), without tipping her upper body forward, and so on.

Each instructor has his own ways of helping children to improve their flat work to the point where they can begin jumping with safety. Stretching and balancing exercises, variously using one rein or none, and games like "follow the leader" can liven up children's lessons and help break the monotony of trotting and cantering around the ring. Many instructors also want their young riders to be able to ride without stirrups, certainly a safety feature if, over a jump or even on the flat, your child inadvertently loses one or both stirrups.

Every instructor is also guided by his own particular criteria and sense of when a youngster is ready to begin jumping. He has been watching your child's riding improve over several months now and has been listening, as well. And what he has heard this time confirms what he knows to be true: Children let you know when they are ready to try jumping, through their words and actions.

Beginner Jumps

Initially, your child will jump the simplest and smallest of fences. In fact, as mentioned before, she'll undoubtedly start by trotting over ground poles, which are jump poles that have been laid on the ground at various points in the ring. She'll do this, with heels down, eyes up, body inclined slightly forward, hands steady on the reins or, perhaps, grabbing a clump of mane, until she feels comfortable enough to try her first jump, a very low crossrail.

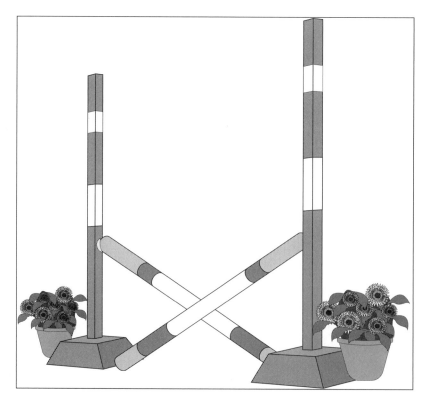

Crossrail.

In time, the crossrail is raised a notch or two, and a second jump is introduced: a straight rail, a low upright made of a single pole suspended between two jump standards. The obstacles, each to be jumped separately, are positioned in the ring so that the rider has ample space to trot into the individual jump and away from it.

The children circle the ring, following each other over the jumps, looking more and more comfortable in their forward position, called the half seat, or two-point. The horses are completely willing, most of them having had years of practice, and all of them look like it is almost as much fun for them as it is for the riders.

These simple training fences are the sum of her experience until, by her performance if not her actual words, she tells the instructor that she is ready to try something more.

Many jumps await her and her horse, all of modest height for the immediate future. Without being so imposing as to frighten either of them, a variety of fences can challenge rider and horse, helping to build the confidence and ability needed so that one day they will be able to handle any obstacle. Now is when the saying "Throw your heart over the fence, and your horse will follow" starts to make sense!

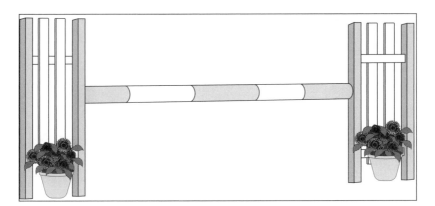

Straight rail.

Throw Your Heart over the Fence . . .

An old-fashioned saying proclaims "Throw your heart over the fence, and your horse will follow." How true that is! A rider must approach a fence as committed to going over it herself as she wants her horse to be. Her total being—head, heart, and body—must transmit confidently "We're all set. Go for it" to the horse. Even at this very early stage, this commitment is something for your child to think about.

However, if a rider heads toward a jump saying to herself, "Oh, no, I don't want to do this," her body language will reflect her hesitation, and the horse will sense it. He, too, becomes uncertain. "Well, kid," he thinks to himself, "you're in charge here. If you don't want to take this jump, I guess I don't, either." And with that, he may refuse the jump by stopping dead in front of it or doing what is called "running out," dodging away from the fence to the left or right. Either way is disconcerting, especially to a beginning rider, who is just learning how to position her body for a jump. She is not as steady on the horse as she will be with more experience, and when the horse abruptly alters his forward motion, your child may get pitched forward or flung to one side or the other, and perhaps onto the ground. If this happens regularly, your child's self-confidence can be shaken.

School horses, it should be remembered, are very well trained, but they are not robots. They are wonderful teachers because if a beginning rider asks for something in the proper manner by employing the correct aids (as she has been taught), the horse will respond appropriately. But approaching a jump with uncertainty sends mixed signals and can confuse even the best schoolie.

Understanding Jumping

A fence is a fence, you thought: two uprights with a pole suspended between them. And then you got a look at the array of jumps in the ring, all different and angled every which way. What a sight!

Different fences are designed to present different challenges. For example, consider these three fences: a simple straight rail, blue and white striped, with a white ground pole beneath; a flat panel painted red and black and standing on edge; and a white chicken coop, made of two panels leaning against each other to form, from the side view, an A-frame. Although they are all the same height (2 feet), each creates a different visual problem to rider or horse that may or may not affect their performance together. With training and practice, however, both of them will become adept enough to jump any fence within their range of ability, no matter how it looks. And with even more seasoning, the pair will be equally unflappable at a horse show, where they will be seeing new fences in different combinations.

Fences are generally made of wood and, in most instances, some parts of them break away on impact. Poles, the easiest to dislodge, rest in shallow metal cups attached to the inner edge of each standard and can be knocked out of the cups with a fairly light tap.

Because jumps can be expensive, especially the number needed to set up a course, stables frequently create their own for training purposes. A couple of oil drums, painted bright colors and laid on their sides, end to end, or pieces of colorful carpeting thrown over a straight rail, can serve very nicely. And paint, of course, can work wonders. Though anything goes, intense primary and secondary colors with black and a great deal of white are the most popular choice. Fake flowers, shrubbery, strips of triangular plastic flags last seen at a store's grand opening, and other decorations can add to the visual challenge without increasing the height of a fence.

Hunters, Jumpers, and Eventers

Most fences are derivatives of natural obstacles found in fields—hay bales, logs on the ground, boundary fences—that riders will encounter while out with the hunt or simply a pleasure ride. In competition, English hunt seat riders jump prescribed courses, set up in arenas for hunters and jumpers and set up cross-country for that event. Many horses are "typey" and acquit themselves better in one way of going or another, but others perform admirably in different jumping disciplines.

At the beginning level, horses are simply jumping fences, without the need to distinguish between types. But as the jumps get higher, horses tend to show what they do best. In general, horses over fences look their part:

- Hunters have a calm, relaxed, elegant way of going. They cover the ground with long, even strides and take their fences in the same measured, unflappable manner. They look like they could go all day on the hunt field and, indeed, that's what they were originally meant to do. Thoroughbreds and warm bloods are popular hunter types.

- Jumpers are agile, powerful horses who are more spirited in their way of going than others. They are more

Designing, building, and painting jumps—and repainting them after a year's wear and tear—are all stable routines that riders frequently help with. Getting together for a painting party followed by pizza or a barbecue can be a lot of fun, as is setting up and testing the new jumps the next day.

Virtually any fence seen at a horse show, including those used at the grand prix level, can be scaled down in size for a beginning jumper. Not every stable has the resources to have a great many jumps, of course, but to the extent that the stable can provide compact than hunters, with short backs and powerful haunches. And they are both speedy and maneuverable. They can be any breed, but the best of them have a "let me at 'em" attitude about jumps.

- Eventers are triple-threat horses, able to gallop cross-country over fixed, sturdy, natural-looking obstacles; jump a course of fences in an arena; and execute a dressage test. They must be strong, fit, and bold, with the stamina and obedience to perform in all three disciplines. At the lower levels, the three competitions are scheduled in one day; at the upper levels, they are spread out, thus the name three-day event.

With few exceptions, hunters and jumpers jump essentially the same type of fences at horse shows. However, both the layout of the courses and the performance asked of the horses are different from and reflect these horses' inherent ways of going. Hunters, moving in an even, rhythmic way, jump courses of fences laid out for them to show these qualities. Jumpers, in contrast, go faster, turn tighter, and jump combinations of fences that show off what quick, powerful, bold horses they can be.

them, it will benefit the riders. After all, it is exciting for youngsters to try their skills on a variety of challenges. If these children do decide to show, when they come face to face with similar jumps in the show ring, they will be that much more confident, having seen them before.

VERTICALS AND SPREADS

Despite their imaginative color combinations and configurations, and modest or imposing size, jumps fall into two categories:

uprights or verticals, which are fences constructed in a single vertical plane, and spreads or horizontals, which are fences built of parallel elements. Some jumps, as you might imagine, combine elements of both vertical and horizontal fences. Most of them match their names quite well.

Typical vertical fences are all embellishments of the upright principle: panels, gates, expanses of low stockade fencing between two standards, and anything else that is essentially about height rather than breadth. Spread fences are the opposite: They are constructed of two or more elements that create a wide jump, from takeoff to landing point. Typical examples are parallel bars and oxers.

Other fences present a more complex picture for horse and rider. Rolltops, for instance, are certainly spreads. But with their solid and rather curious appearance, the message they send to horse and rider is that this requires a bold, no-nonsense effort, or, as the horse might say to himself, "I'm not sure what this is, but I don't want to hit it." The same can be said for other formidable-looking jumps. Walls and wishing wells, for example, are uprights. They are actually constructed of plywood but made to look substantial, and horses jump them as if they are.

As fence heights increase, uprights and spreads, by their very nature, test different qualities in horse and rider. Uprights test the high-jumping ability of the horse. They are more difficult fences to jump because the pair must determine by themselves the take-off spot in front of the jump. Spreads, which challenge a horse to stretch out over a jump, are the more natural type because, in a general sense, they conform to the horse's own bodily arc over the fence. They are also easier to jump because the takeoff spot is more apparent since it is fairly close to the most forward element of the jump.

For now, the small versions of any fence that your child will jump all have the same objective: to teach her to ride a horse over a fence with the same confidence she now has riding on the flat. Her trusted school horse has jumped all the jumps countless times and, at a beginner's low height, takes the uprights and spreads with equal ease.

COMMON FENCE TYPES

The following are some of the most popular jumps you will see, beginning at your home stable and, later, in the show ring. They are arranged, loosely, in order of their difficulty, although of course, no such arrangement is absolute. The simplest, low crossrails and straight rails, are discussed earlier in this chapter. After them, the jumps that your trainer will use, and the order in which he introduces them, will depend on what he finds most beneficial in building a young jumper's confidence.

An oxer is a spread fence constructed of two horizontal bars, each attached to a separate standard. The forward bar is lower than the one behind. In the case of a Swedish oxer, the two bars are slanted in opposite directions. As horse and rider approach, the fence appears like a shallow crossrail suspended in air.

With parallel bars, the top bar in each plane is the same height.

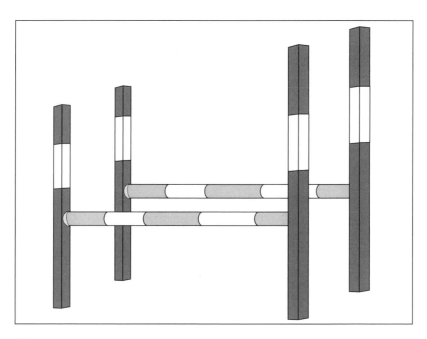

Oxer.

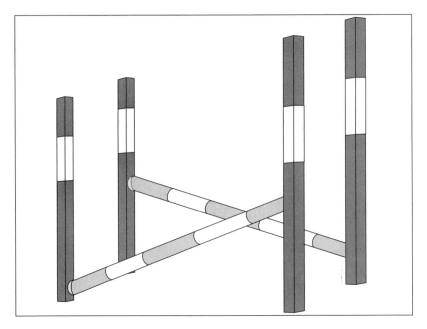

Swedish oxer.

In a triple bar, the three bars are arranged in ascending height. Because a horse's jump (also known as his arc, or bascule) naturally follows such an upward curvature, this is one of the easiest fences to take.

A hogsback, another type of spread fence, looks like a regular oxer from either direction. Between and parallel to the other two poles, there is a single higher center pole. It can also be solidly constructed to look like a miniature barn. What was the high, center pole is now the ridgeline of the roof. This style of hogsback is most often found on a cross-country course.

A brush box is a rectangular structure, rather like a giant window box. It usually has shrubbery coming out of the top, and it can have a parallel rail above it. The dimensions can be anywhere from a low of 6 inches to 2 feet or higher, and it can be just a few inches deep to the thickness of a hedge. With a small, narrow brush box, it's not much of a spread, but with a bigger, deeper box, the spread element is enhanced.

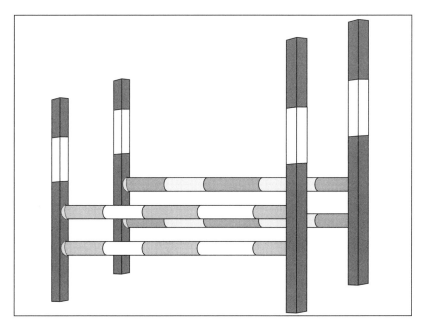

Parallel bars.

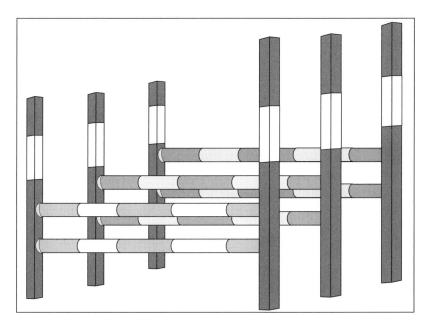

Triple bar.

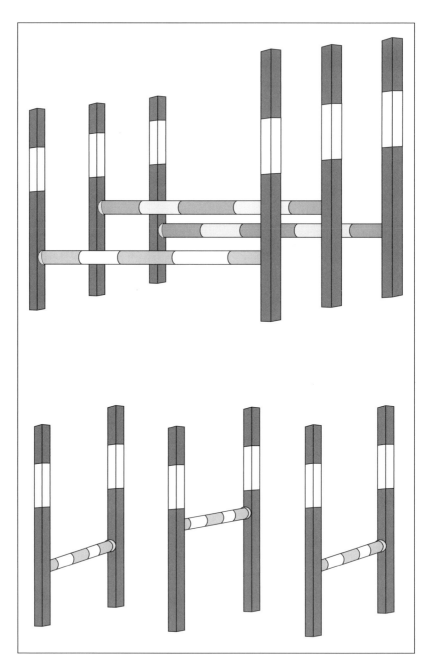

Hogsback.

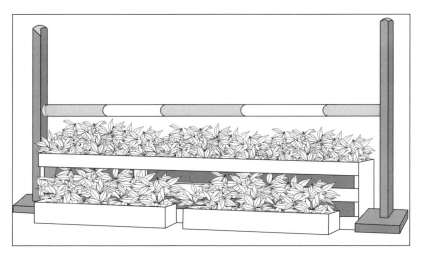

Brush box.

A panel is a good example of a vertical fence. It can be a solid panel or one that looks like a picket or stockade fence, or it can be another design that embodies similar characteristics. It can have a single rail, or more, set above the panel.

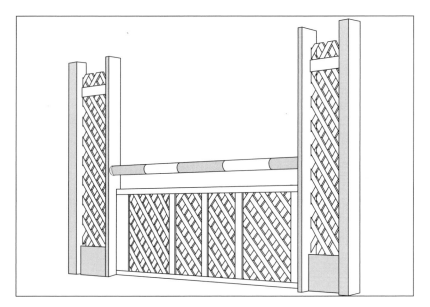

Panel.

A wall looks just like its name, although the gray "fieldstone" or red "brick" is actually painted on plywood boards. Rather than conventional standards, it probably has "stone" pillars at each side. This and other solid-looking fences can actually be more appealing to horses than the more obvious upright-type jump with poles. Because of their substantial appearance, horses usually make a better effort in jumping them.

The chicken coop, or coop, has flat sides that are angled so that they meet in a single ridge along the top like an A-frame. Like brush boxes, walls, and other panels, a coop is a typical hunter fence, adapted from those found in the hunt field.

A rolltop resembles a longitudinal quarter of a giant cylinder, with the curved outside edge facing the approaching horse and rider. It is usually covered in bright green shag carpeting to make it look like a grassy knoll. A rolltop is generally about 2.5 feet at its highest point. After a horse gets used to seeing it, this is technically an easy jump for him because it matches his body's natural arc in the air.

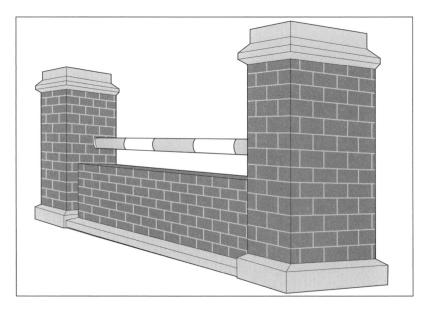

Wall.

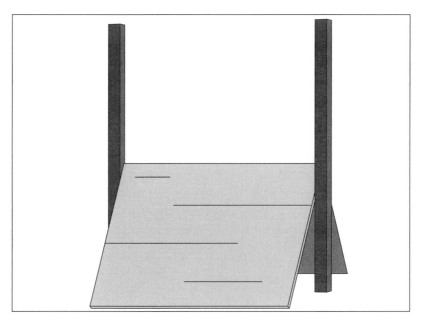

Chicken coop.

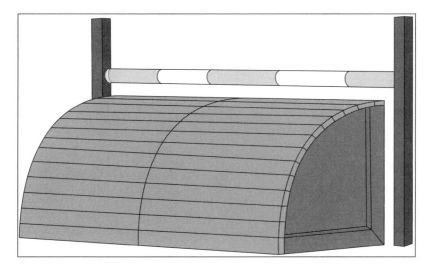

Rolltop.

A bank is a mound of dirt, rather like a ledge or a plateau, large enough that the horse jumps on and off it. One side usually is a more moderate grade than the other. At a show, such a jump is only going to be found where the show grounds are a permanent outdoor facility. Usually it is found on a cross-country course.

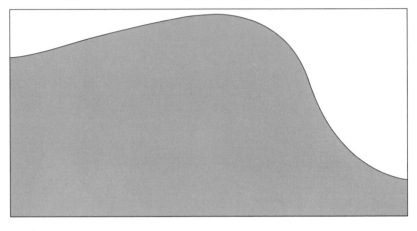

Bank.

A bouncer consists of two fences set close enough together so that the horse jumps in over the first fence, rocks back on his haunches, and jumps out over the second fence without taking a full stride. It is, therefore, also called a no-stride.

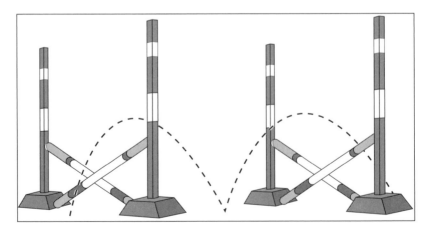

Bouncer.

An in-and-out is another combination of two fences, this time with enough space between the two uprights so that a horse has room to jump in, take one full stride, and then jump out. It also derives from the hunt, during which the horses jumped the fence out of one field, crossed the country road in a stride, and jumped the fence into the next field.

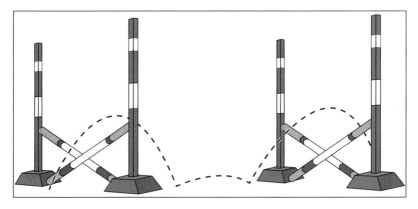

In-and-out.

A gymnastic is three or more fences set up as a series. It is an excellent training device for both rider and horse—to help the rider improve her balance and position, and to help the horse improve his balance, pace, and use of his body. Such a setup can be tight, requiring a horse to shorten his strides, or long, forcing him to open up, or lengthen, his strides. It's a good at-home fence and can also be found at shows.

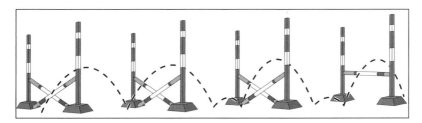

Gymnastic.

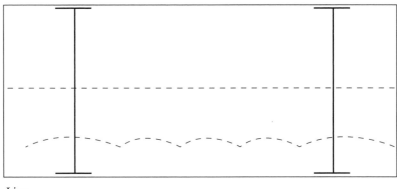

Line.

A line is the straight path through the center of a fence. The approach can be a perpendicular line or a diagonal line. Also, when two jumps are set in relation to each other, in a straight line and a measured distance apart, they are called a line. The distance is set in horse strides, commonly between three and six, although longer distances often show up on outdoor courses. A broken line also refers to two jumps that are set in relation to each other, but with a path between them that is curved rather than straight.

A liverpool, a water jump, is a shallow, rectangular pool of water usually combined with a low straight-rail fence, either at the take-off side or across the middle of the water. On a cross-country course, it is natural looking, whereas as a training fence or in a stadium competition it is a human-made rectangle, colored blue on the inside and filled with water. It is a more advanced type of spread fence, complicated by the visual challenge of ripples and light reflecting off the water. It must be jumped in one stride, without the horse's feet touching the water on either side.

Particularly at shows, you will see other jumps, most of them variations on those described here. With this as a guide, however, it should be pretty easy to figure out what your young rider and her horse, as well as others at the show, will have to do to negotiate any jump successfully.

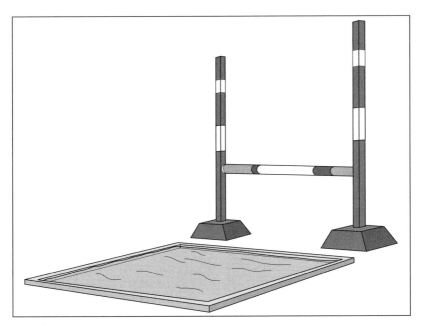

Liverpool.

When to Slow the Pace

As your child begins jumping, she is likely to enjoy herself immensely. But what if things start to change?

Some children improve faster than the others, and they may become impatient with the little fences. They want to try bigger fences and combinations of two or more, which is the start of what they would be doing in jumping a course. And, indeed, some of them are ready to move on before others. But perhaps your child isn't ready for more yet.

It is certainly not a clear-cut situation. Some children move themselves along, always ambitious to try the next step. Others are slower and may need to be prodded now and then to help them advance. Crossrails and low straight rails can become very easy. Even the tiniest pony has to do little more than a hop to get himself and his rider over one of these.

When the jumps get higher and more imposing, your child may begin to look reluctant. You can read the doubt on her face. She seems hesitant to go over these bigger fences, scared while she is doing it, and never pleased and relaxed afterward. It would appear that she is being overfaced—that is, pushed to jump higher than she is, at this point, comfortable doing. She keeps trying because the others in her class are jumping the bigger fences, but she doesn't seem to be gaining confidence. In fact, it looks like just the opposite is happening.

This is an instance, before things really start to slide backward, when it's time to have a talk with the instructor. You need to tell him how the situation appears to you and ask his opinion. As with other times when your child has run into trouble, if your budget can handle a few private lessons, that may be the answer. Then, without the pressure of other riders doing better than she, your child may be able to bolster her confidence. Or again, there may be another group of riders who are still working with lower fences that she can join. She will feel secure again. Then she will get bored when these lower fences get too easy and will be ready to try the higher ones once more, this time better prepared.

Again, it's important to let your child set the pace. Given the chance, children are pretty forthright about what they want to do. Some are perfectly happy, for the foreseeable future, just jumping small fences. Others' eyes start to sparkle when they contemplate bigger ones. One way is as good as the next. It is just one of the many choices riding has to offer your child.

Chapter Eight

Your Dedicated Rider

*W*ill you take me down to the barn, please?" This, from your child, is now one of the most frequently asked questions around the house, easily as popular as "What's for dinner?"

It is increasingly apparent that your youngster would rather ride than do just about anything else. She will go down to the stable every day after school, if you will take her, and spend all of Saturday and Sunday there, too. She thinks nothing of riding in all types of weather, save a downpour or a blizzard. After telling yourself, on any given day, that she won't ride long because it is getting dark and you're sure she is tired and hungry, you finally have to tell her point-blank to get off the horse. If you don't, she will just keep riding, and you will never get home.

She is willing to do anything to help out around the barn: groom horses, sweep the aisles, cool off hot horses by walking them around before they go back to their stalls, set jumps—you name it. And whenever the instructor or the stable manager says, "No one has ridden what's-his-name today. Why don't you hop on and give him some exercise?" your child's eyes light up.

Despite their obvious and enormous differences from one another, children and horses often develop the most amazing rapport, to the awe and delight of onlookers. Just like people, horses warm to affection and attention, and they respond in kind.

In case you hadn't fully realized it, far beyond liking horses, your child has become totally captivated by them. At a stable, among friends and friendly horses, she has found a home away from home.

Living with a Rider in the Family

You've noticed bits of hay everywhere—in the rugs, in your child's bed, and even on your favorite stuffed chair. And some of it is clumped together with bits of mud or, oh, dear, *is that manure*? So it goes, even though the new house rule of leaving riding boots in the front hall is reasonably well obeyed.

Horse books are a recent addition to your child's library, as are some riding magazines. And among the pictures taped to her bedroom walls are a growing collection of some very beautiful horses.

Her birthday wish list is strictly equipment, riding apparel, and other horsey items. It makes for one-stop shopping, and you can direct anyone asking you for gift suggestions to the nearest tack shop.

SUPPORT FROM THE WHOLE FAMILY

Everywhere, there are signs of your youngster's deepening commitment to the sport. Riding is now becoming important enough to her that she is willing to make her own adjustments and sacrifices so that she can increase her involvement. To do it, of course, she needs your continued interest and support and, hopefully, that of the rest of the family. If you haven't done it before, now is a good time to encourage your partner and any other children in the family to come to the stable on occasion.

Whether or not everyone stands around and watches a full lesson should depend on how your child feels about the idea. Nevertheless, the whole family's interest in seeing what their young rider has accomplished, as well as where she spends so much of her time and energy, is important. And realizing how much fun she is having may give a sibling the encouragement to try riding, too.

ARE *YOU* HOLDING UP OKAY?

For someone who never spent any time around horses, things have certainly changed for you. Not only are you around them a good bit now, but you are actually feeling very comfortable with them. In fact, when someone asks, "Will you hold my horse for a minute?" you do so without batting an eye.

What's more, the other day your child said, "Hey, Mom, want to try my horse? Why don't you get on him and just walk around a little?" (after asking the instructor if it would be all right, of course). And do you know what? The idea didn't throw you into an absolute tailspin. True, you didn't take her up on it. But who knows? Someday you might.

Hopefully, you are making some new friends yourself, such as other parents with whom to compare notes and share a laugh over your new experiences. When your exasperation level is running high because it feels like all you are doing is running a chauffeuring service to and from the stable, and your other errands seem to be getting lost in the shuffle, it helps to know you are not the only one to whom this is happening. Besides, you may find a willing partner to share the driving detail, which will give you both more time to do other things.

Increasing Benefits of Riding

The notion that riding could be "something to do once in a while" is long gone, replaced by what may be your child's first wholehearted involvement in an activity outside the home. Her early efforts have been rewarded, and she has become a pretty decent novice rider, able to hold her own among the other riders of her level at the stable. Happy with her accomplishments, she is anxious to press on.

Riding is giving her focus, direction, and goals. She now understands enough of the techniques and skills required to appreciate what more advanced riders have achieved. In fact, she is beginning to picture herself as one of them. You are probably hearing it in conversation—how she is going to become one of the best riders at the stable, go to shows, jump big fences, and win blue ribbons. Or be an event rider. Or own a champion cutting horse. Or barrel race. Or just become an all-around great rider. Whatever her hopes, she is starting to really believe in herself and her abilities.

It is nice for you to see, too, that your child is developing skills in a sport that she can continue to enjoy throughout her life. As her abilities improve and she begins to direct her energies to particular facets of riding, she will discover that it is at once exciting and relaxing, solitary and good fun in a group, never dull, and always changing. And even though the sport is becoming increasingly popular, knowing how to ride is still considered special, something not everyone learns how to do.

Keeping Watch over Schoolwork

You may well have your own words to add here and there, but in short order, you will probably be saying something like, "There are only twenty-four hours in the day. You can't do everything. But one of the things you *will* do is your schoolwork."

Chances are your youngster already has a routine for doing her homework, as you have your way of checking that it gets done. Depending on her age and aptitude, you know how much time and effort must be spent, which subjects are easy for her, and which take more work.

Now riding has entered the picture, taking up several hours a week. Each lesson leaves your child exhilarated but also probably tired and, on a school day, a little less inclined to do her assignments when she gets home. All too easily, grades can start to slide. It's better to set some ground rules up front than wait until a poor report card is brought home. However you want to handle it, you need to make it clear that schoolwork is at the top of the list and that riding comes after.

You will find that most riding instructors are very supportive of such a position and will be glad to help you by reminding young riders that if they don't keep their grades up, they may not be able to continue riding. Again, it will be up to you to set the guidelines and be firm about them so that a balance is maintained between riding, schoolwork, and the other things your child must do.

At times, if the involvement in riding gets excessive, you may have to enforce a cutback. While eliminating riding completely until schoolwork picks up might provoke resentment and actually worsen the situation, cutting back for the time being could have a positive effect.

As a suggestion, limit riding to Fridays, Saturdays, Sundays, and holidays until schoolwork improves. When grades are back up and you are reasonably confident that they will stay that way, as a reward you can let your child resume riding more often. When she knows you are serious about schoolwork coming first, you may not have to make the point a second time.

Equipment Considerations at This Point

At this point, all additional equipment besides a schooling helmet and shoes, including a saddle, is still optional. But depending on the type of stable you go to and what things the other children are getting, it could well be the right time to buy certain items.

IS IT TIME FOR A SADDLE?

Besides riding apparel, a saddle is the most personal item a rider can own. It is sized to fit her own anatomical seat and, if purchased new, will be broken in to correspond to the way she sits a horse and rides. Whether it is an English or Western saddle, the proper selection can increase riding comfort and effective communication with the horse.

Perhaps because a saddle is the single most expensive item in riding, except for the horse himself, having your own saddle says you are a serious, committed rider. Children are just as desirous of this mark of a rider as anyone else, and prodded by peer pressure, at some point each child will start to think about having her own saddle. As a practical matter at shows, and at the stable, too, it means that your child never has to wait for a saddle. When a horse is available, she can tack up and be ready to go. Depending on family finances, this may be the time for you to give it some serious consideration.

Saddles come in a wide range of prices and quality. Fine, custom-made ones can run a few thousand dollars. Most leather English saddles from well-known manufacturers are made in England, Germany, and France and, with today's climbing prices, you will pay several hundred dollars even for a child's model, including findings (that is, stirrups, stirrups leathers, and a girth). Saddles made elsewhere are less costly, as are those made of synthetic materials. One of the latter, for a child, will cost in the $200 range. Because, if she continues to ride, a child is probably going to outgrow whatever saddle is bought now, buying a less expensive saddle might make sense. Western saddles are still mostly manufactured in the United States, and there are many custom-made models to be had. Overall, their prices are much the same as for English saddles.

If you can find one in good condition, you might also consider a used saddle, which will cost considerably less than a new one. It may come stripped of findings, so you will have to purchase those separately. Whatever your choice, new or used, encourage your child to take care of her saddle (with your help, if need be).

Used saddles are already conditioned, but if you purchase a new one, it will have to be well conditioned before your child uses it. Your trainer and other experienced riders at the stable can tell you exactly what to do. Beyond that, good continuing care is key to the longevity of all things leather. At minimum, you'll need a couple small tack sponges and a bar of glycerin soap, and after each ride, your youngster should be encouraged to lightly clean her saddle, so there will be no buildup of sweat and dirt. Other leather products are useful, too, and again, you can find what you need from a tack shop or catalog source. The main thing is to get your youngster in the habit of taking care of her equipment. Then, when she outgrows the saddle, you will be able to resell it and recoup a good part of your investment.

Before you actually purchase a saddle, talk to people with experience and see what is around. If other children at the stable already have their own saddles, your child should ask if she can try them to see how they feel to her. Tack shops will also let you sit in saddles, and some will even let you take one to the stable to see how it feels on a horse's back. If you do, you may be asked to try it without stirrups, so as not to mark up the flaps.

Tack shop personnel are usually quite knowledgeable about saddles. Ask your riding instructor's advice, too. Along with everything else you need, saddles can also be purchased through a catalog or online. If you go this route, your child won't have the advantage of sitting in the saddle before you purchase it. But if you follow the dealer's instructions about trying it out once received, it should be returnable if it is the wrong choice.

Among the tack suppliers listed in chapter 5 (see the sidebar "Tack Suppliers") are several with good selections of saddles, both English and Western. Now is a good time to get familiar with what is available and what such a purchase is likely to cost.

As you do your homework, bear in mind that the choice of a saddle is a very individual matter. You will soon find out that what feels wonderful to one rider can be uncomfortable to another. Fortunately, though, your young rider's taste is not too highly developed yet. Should you decide that it is time for a saddle, whether ultimately the decision is to look for used or buy new, an educated choice, in the proper size, will undoubtedly make her very happy.

ADDITIONAL EQUIPMENT TO CONSIDER NOW

Especially if your child rides one or two school horses all the time and has become very attached to them, you may want to get her some grooming tools so that she can take special care of "her" horses. A couple of brushes—one with stiff bristles, the other soft—and a rub rag or two (your old terry cloth hand towels), a hoof pick, body sponge, sweat scraper, fly spray, and hoof dressing are possibilities, along with a grooming box or caddy in which to carry them.

Buying a Used Saddle

If you want a used saddle, see if local tack shops have any on consignment. Also check bulletin boards at tack shops, feed stores, and stables (your own and neighboring stables) to see what is being sold privately. The local horseman's association in your area, or other organization, may also run a tack swap night once or twice a year, and you may find something there. And don't be shy about mentioning to friends and others in your horse community that you're looking for a used child's saddle. Some teenager may still have hers stashed in the basement and would be happy to sell it.

Of course, there are also the classifieds in your local general newspaper and in the local horseman's newspaper (if one is published for your area). Local horseman's newspapers are usually free and can be found on the counter at your local feed or tack store.

Online, check eBay (www.ebay.com). Some of the tack suppliers listed in chapter 5 may also have used saddles at times, so inquire.

Some stables make room for regular students to store their equipment on the premises, even if they don't have their own horses. If so, a small tack trunk, such as a camp footlocker or a heavy-duty plastic box with a hinged lid, is another worthwhile purchase now. Better yet, check your attic or neighborhood tag sales; a used trunk, with a coat of paint, if you like, makes a perfect tack trunk. And you won't feel so bad when you see how banged up it can get at the stable.

Chapter Nine

Getting Involved in Horse Shows

*I*f you haven't been to a show by now, look around. Sometime soon there is bound to be one at a stable near you. While you can still be a truly casual spectator, with nothing more pressing to do than enjoy the sights, sounds, and a sizzling hot dog and a soft drink, why not take the family and see what shows are all about? Depending on the size of the show, there may be an entry fee, but the smallest schooling shows are usually free.

Each year there are literally thousands of horse shows throughout the country. They range from small, informal schooling shows that draw horses and riders from neighboring stables and nearby backyards, to major events of several days' duration in New York City and Lake Placid, New York; Denver; Washington, D.C.; Devon, Pennsylvania; Palm Beach and Gainesville, Florida; and elsewhere, at which horses and riders from all over the United States and other countries compete.

Quite naturally, shows in a given geographic area offer what competitors there want. Thus, you will find more hunter-jumper-equitation shows in the East, competitions for three- and five-gaited Saddlebred horses in the South, and shows catering to Western stock seat riders in the West. Then again, there will be Western shows in the East, hunter-jumper shows in the West, Saddlebred shows in the Midwest, and dressage shows throughout the country.

Big or small, shows can be as festive as a country fair and as exciting as any spectator sport. Whether you are outdoors with action going on in four or five rings spread over several grassy acres or in one ring in the center of the stable grounds, or indoors with spectators sitting or standing all around the arena's edge, horse shows are colorful, lively, eye-filling events.

Riders and horses, all looking their polished best, are everywhere. Following them, an assortment of friends and relatives are ready to rebraid manes, toss on coolers, whisper words of encouragement, and hold the ribbons won. Over the public address system, a voice calls riders to their next class, announces winners of one just finished, and implores forgetful riders to come and sign their otherwise complete entry forms.

No matter the show's size, the atmosphere is much the same, tingling with nervousness and laughter, frustration and exuberance. Horses know as well as their riders that they are at a show, and the challenge to the riders is to perform their best and help their horses do the same.

A show takes work, but when it all comes together, and the judge walks over and hands a rider a ribbon, there is no denying the feeling of pride and accomplishment. You will see it on your child's face the day her number is called and a ribbon is handed to her.

Is Showing for Your Child?

There is a lot to be gained from showing. So should your child go to shows? The simple answer is probably yes, to the extent that you should at least give horse shows a try. The better answer, understandably, is more complex. That is, yes, if your child wants to show and is ready, and if you, who knows her best, think it's the right thing to do and the right time to do it.

How the situation has changed! When you and your child first came to the stable, thoughts of competing at a horse show sailed right over your heads. That was a long way off, if ever, you thought. The first thing was to learn how to ride.

Now, many months and many accomplishments later, the question of going to a horse show has some validity, especially with the buzz around your stable about an upcoming show. "Are you showing next weekend?" you've heard more than one youngster say excitedly to another.

And then, lo and behold, the instructor raises the question with you: How would you feel about your child participating at this upcoming show? Chances are it will be a small show, he points out, one that will attract horses and riders from your stable and a couple of other local stables, plus a few more stabled in area backyards. It shouldn't be very crowded, not much pressure, and it could be a lot of fun. Just the sort of situation you want for a first show, he adds.

Youngsters in the stable's beginner riding program, like your child, don't have their own horses. So when any of them go to a show, they take one of the school horses. If you decide to do this, you pay the stable a day rental fee for the horse. It shouldn't be a lot, but the fee is management's decision, so the best thing to do is ask about it up front. If there are more kids going to a show than school horses for kids who need them, the kids will share horses. This can work nicely—if your child and another share a horse, you will only pay half the rental fee, as well as half the cost of vanning the horse to the show. There are other fees involved in showing, as discussed later in the chapter. But suffice it to say that at this point the logistics of going to a show are simple, and essentially everything is arranged for you.

"Well, why not?" you think? Or, on second thought, "Why?" After all, things have been going along very nicely as is. Your youngster has been enjoying her lessons and spending time at the barn. She has made some friends and learned a lot about horses. Is it really necessary to start going to horse shows? "Things could stay just the way they are," you reason with yourself, privately wondering, "Why rock the boat?"

And, indeed, leaving things the way they are can be just fine. There are no hard-and-fast rules in horseback riding that say, for example, that once you become proficient at the walk, trot, and canter, the next step has to be learning how to jump fences. Or, if you ride Western, that once you master the jog and lope you should take up barrel racing. And that whatever you do, eventually you have to go to shows and compete against other riders.

Instinctively, your sense may be that this is enough for now, that it would be the wrong thing to ask your child to do at this point. Perhaps both of you will agree that simply learning how to ride and your child's enjoying herself as much as she is doing are quite enough for now. One of the beauties of riding is that when you have become comfortable on a horse and have learned how to walk, trot, and canter with security, there are many avenues open to you, not the least of which is going out for a leisurely trail ride.

Nevertheless, for many beginning riders, going to horse shows is an exciting next step. And if you and your youngster are ready, there is much to recommend the experience, and there are many benefits to be realized. Reaching the point where your young rider feels ready to go to her first show is a milestone that you and your child can be proud of. From that first lesson, when she learned how to get on and off a horse, hold the reins, turn left and right, walk and stop, to the point where she can go into a show ring and hold her own is a big accomplishment. If she ever once said to herself, "I'll never get that good," she is now ready to take her turn.

The idea of going to a show is infectious, especially when what you are considering is a small, relaxed show in which lots of beginning riders will participate. After all, if the other children are going, why shouldn't your child? From your standpoint, if the cost of showing will preclude doing much of it, an occasional nonrated schooling show, with lower entry fees than at the bigger shows, may be a way to let her try her hand once in a while and not feel completely left out.

It bears saying, though, that while horse shows appeal to a great many people, they are not everyone's cup of tea. For whatever reason, some children—and, indeed, riders of any age—try showing but just never take a liking to it. So be it. If this is the situation with your child, allow her to find her niche elsewhere in the sport and not feel any less capable because showing isn't it.

The important thing is whether she *wants* to show. As she has done before, your child will let you know whether and when she's ready. However, if she is hesitant but your gut feeling is that she really would like to begin showing, you as her parent will know best how much encouraging or prodding is appropriate. Instructors, too, can be very good at persuading a reluctant youngster, maybe by suggesting that she go to a couple shows as a sort of trial run and see how she feels after that. Kids have a lot of fun at shows, and you wouldn't want your child to wind up feeling left out when all she needed was a little nudge in the direction of the show grounds!

More Than Ribbons: Benefits of Shows

Horse shows can give children a chance to compete in a good sense of the word by trying their best and taking pride in their individual achievements, whether or not they are rewarded with a ribbon. With the instructor's help, a child can learn to set goals that are within her reach, be they keeping her horse cantering

Good Sportsmanship

Part of a winning package, even when your child doesn't take home a ribbon, is watching her behave in a sportsmanlike manner. It's something you can help her to learn. As needed, remind her of the following:

- Always reward your horse. He's tried his best.

- Congratulate riders who won ribbons when you didn't or who placed higher than you did.

- Thank those who helped you get through the day: your trainer, other riders, and your parents.

- Keep a positive attitude and consider each show as a step in the right direction (progress or a specific goal).

- Learn something at each show that you can build on for the next time.

without a break, jumping all the fences without a refusal, or just sitting up straight and keeping her heels down and her hands steady. And, oh, what music to her instructor's ears when, back at the stable, she says that next time she will canter better or keep her lower leg still, or makes other such positive decisions.

Showing can help your child develop poise and confidence. It will also teach her to cope with nervousness by learning to work through it and continuing to perform. Unlike riding in a lesson, when a problem can be immediately addressed, in a show she has to learn to deal with the unexpected without much handholding from her instructor. And what she'll find out, hopefully, is that she is doing pretty well.

Horse shows are also the perfect place to learn sportsmanship, and you and your child's instructor can work together to encourage a good attitude. Nothing can spoil the day for bystanders and other participants as quickly as ill-behaving children, those who whine and sulk when they don't ride well and who blame the horse and everybody else for anything that goes wrong. What brightens the day for everyone is children who are enjoying themselves, doing the best they can, and, even at this young age, learning to applaud and congratulate each other for their accomplishments.

Types of Shows

By now you have probably heard the terms *recognized show* and, conversely, *unrecognized* or *schooling show*, and you are beginning to realize that more new vocabulary awaits you, just when you were feeling pretty secure in your knowledge of riding terms.

Well, fear not, this, too, will make sense soon enough. The United States Equestrian Federation (USEF), the national governing body for equestrian sport in the United States, sanctions competitions for twenty-seven disciplines and breeds. The organizers of an upcoming USEF-recognized show agree to meet all USEF standards for that particular competition and in so doing must abide by the organization's rules. As an indication of the numbers and diversity of equine sports, USEF, while the largest organization, is only one of several overseeing recognized competitions, and it rewards top performers with year-end and other awards. Concern with such awards is a long way off for your child. But getting to know some of the associations that are influential to the sport may be beneficial even now.

Recognized shows are generally larger than unrecognized ones, attended by more riders and horses, and offer more classes (that is, the individual competitions that riders enter at a show). Every year across the country, major shows are held for each of several disciplines, among them equitation, hunters and jumpers, dressage, and Western, and for breeds such as Arabian, Morgan, and Saddlebred. Many other competitions are open to more than one of the foregoing categories.

But in all likelihood, what concerns you at this early stage in your child's riding are schooling, or unrecognized, shows. They are almost always smaller and subject to less hustle and bustle than their recognized counterparts.

At such shows, there should be several classes for young beginning riders, and chances are there won't be too many entrants in each. For a youngster going to her first show, understandably a little nervous and unsure of herself, a show like this is a good way to break in.

These shows also attract riders who are schooling their horses for recognized shows later in the season, or those with "green" horses, who are just starting to go to shows. The atmosphere is more relaxed than that at a recognized show, and while everyone still tries their best, it is understood that many horses and riders are there to learn and improve.

Not only are entry fees lower at schooling shows than at recognized ones, but there are no drug-testing fees for the horses or other extras that are part and parcel of rated shows. So, while your youngster is getting her feet wet, making mistakes, and building confidence, show costs can be kept down.

Another option—small, local, *recognized* shows—don't usually attract a great many competitors either, perhaps because of limited space and facilities. Your instructor will be familiar with the shows in the area, what they have been like in years past, and

Membership Associations

Depending on the extent to which you are a joiner, a number of equine associations may be of interest to you. All have memberships, and you can check to see what category would be most appropriate for your child. Generally, the benefits of membership include subscription to a periodical and other publications, calendars of upcoming shows and other events, as well as information resources. If your child progresses to the point of showing in recognized shows, joining the sanctioning body will also keep entry fees down. The following are some of the most common membership associations in the United States, listed in order of general appeal:

United States Equestrian Federation (USEF)
859-258-2472
www.usef.org

American Quarter Horse Association (AQHA)
806-376-4811
www.aqha.com

American Youth Horse Council
800-TRY-AYHC
www.ayhc.com

United States Pony Clubs, Inc.
859-254-7669
www.ponyclub.org

who has the best selection of classes for the beginning rider to enter. He can guide you as to the best place to begin.

Can You Afford Showing?

Lessons, equipment, and now horse shows? "Whew," you are thinking to yourself, "I can see where this sport can start to run

United States Dressage Federation (USDF)
859-971-2277
www.usdf.org

National Little Britches Rodeo Association (NLBRA)
800-763-3694
www.nlbra.org

National High School Rodeo Association (NHSRA)
800-466-4772
www.nhsra.com

National Reining Horse Association (NRHA)
405-946-7400
www.nrha.com

United States Eventing Association (USEA)
703-779-0440
www.eventingusa.com

American Endurance Ride Conference
866-271-2372
www.aerc.org

American Vaulting Association (AVA)
323-654-0800
www.americanvaulting.org

into a lot of money." And indeed it can, if you don't continue to keep a handle on things.

One of the deciding factors in whether your child participates in shows frequently, occasionally, or not at all is your budget. Like everything else in the sport, showing can cost varying amounts of money, depending on what you and your child would like to do and what you can afford to spend. Having a modest budget doesn't

Show Calendars

With all the disciplines and breeds that compete at shows, and the various organizations that sanction shows, there is, not surprisingly, no one place to go for all upcoming show information. As you begin showing, of course, it's not something you even need to worry about, as your trainer will decide at which shows to compete. But when you want to know what's going on, you can check out *Chronicle of the Horse* (see page 72), a weekly magazine that runs a monthly calendar listing upcoming recognized shows (and some unrecognized shows) in all English hunt seat disciplines except flat racing and polo. It also lists results. In March, it runs an annual calendar for equitation, hunter, and jumper competitions, and in June, it runs an annual dressage competition calendar.

The following are some organizations that list competitions they sanction, both upcoming and results, on their Web sites:

United States Equestrian Federation (USEF)
www.usef.org

American Quarter Horse Association (AQHA)
www.aqha.org

mean that you can't go to *any* shows; it only means that you need to pick and choose. Perhaps you should opt for more of the less expensive, unrecognized shows instead of recognized ones, and pick shows in your area so that the traveling is kept to a minimum.

No matter what, showing does run up the expenses to a greater or lesser degree, and it is something to think about early on, if only in general terms. Before you are to the point of deciding on a particular show, ask your trainer what going to one will cost and look for specifics. Also talk with parents of kids at the stable who are already going to shows. They'll be able to tell you what's in store and, no doubt, share some hard-won know-how.

If your budget can handle whatever comes along, and if your child is interested in showing, then your only concern—and that

United States Dressage Federation (USDF)
www.usdf.org

National Little Britches Rodeo Association (NLBRA)
www.nlbra.org

National High School Rodeo Association (NHSRA)
www.nhsra.org

American Vaulting Association (AVA)
www.americanvaulting.org

For unrecognized, or schooling, shows, you can get more information from local horseman's associations, either county, regional, or state organizations. Most have Web sites and even sponsor shows themselves. Get to know who is active in your area and what they have to offer. The local horseman's newspaper (if there's one in your area), which is free and usually available at feed and tack stores, is also likely to carry show notices.

For breed shows, besides listings with the USEF, contact the organization representing the particular breed.

---

of your instructor—is to send your child to shows that continue to build her confidence and security. But if you have to watch the expenses and you are at a stable that does a lot of showing, it is easy to get swept along, only to realize belatedly that the cost is way beyond your means and, in fact, you are already overbudget.

WHAT FEES ARE INVOLVED?

A home show—that is, a show held at the stable where your child rides—is the least expensive, not to mention the most convenient, place to start. To begin with, the school horse that your child will ride is already on the grounds, thus saving you the cost of having him vanned somewhere else.

Even at your own stable, you can expect a rental fee for using the horse for the day—justified because he will not be available for lessons—but an expense that can be split if your child and another rider will both be showing him. The only wrinkle to this is that, naturally, both riders can't enter the same classes. That's solved by sharing the horse with a rider at a different level, so each will be entering different classes. However, sharing a horse is not always an option, and you should count on it only when it is presented (or you suggest the possibility).

There will also be a fee for braiding the horse's mane, something that's done almost every time you show, whether at home or away. (When your child shares a horse, you split this, too.) Braiding is an elegant touch that makes any horse look very turned out, but it is also a time-consuming job that takes some practice to do well. As an idea for the future, if you or your child learns how to braid, it can save you a few bucks, and if you are ambitious, even make you a little money!

Then there are the entry fees, charged for every class your child rides in at the show. These are paid ahead of time, sent in along with your entry form before the show's closing date. Your instructor will probably collect money and forms and send them in for all his students. While the rules can be more lenient at unrecognized shows, generally speaking, your child will need a bona fide reason for getting fees refunded after she commits to a show. Likewise, she can enter late by paying a late fee, even at the show itself if, for example, things are going well for her and she and her instructor decide to enter another class or two.

Your child will likely ride in two or three classes at a show, based on what she and her instructor think she can handle. If she is age twelve or under, she will be in short stirrup classes along with other kids. Entering one class is hardly worthwhile, given that other expenses will stay the same. The additional classes also provide a cushion in case she was nervous and not up to par in her first ride, as well as a broader base from which to learn. If she will be sharing the school horse with another rider at the show, your instructor will need to balance the horse's total effort with the number of classes he would like each rider to enter. And yes, shows are held rain or shine, although hopefully your child's first show will be on a beautiful, sunny day!

What are you actually paying for, you wonder, as you write a check to the show secretary for this upcoming show? Well, quite simply, you and others like you are paying for the expenses of the show—and to appreciate all the costs involved, put the emphasis on the word *show*. Like any number of other events, such as craft fairs, dog shows, and rock concerts, horse shows take planning, publicity, people in various roles (sometimes paid, sometimes volunteer), props, and start-to-finish direction. Not all expenses arise at every show, but they can include flyers and ads; printing and mailing the program; renting the show grounds, tents, jumps and perimeter fencing, and portable restrooms; hiring a judge for each ring (involves stipend, transportation to the show, and room and board) and the announcer (who will usually furnish a public address system, if the host stable or organization doesn't have one); paying a veterinarian (who will either be on call or actually at the show, depending on its size); a guarantee to the food concessionaire; and ribbons and trophies. Large shows cost more to put on, smaller ones cost less, and in both cases your entry fees, which are scaled to the size of the show, pay the bills.

Certainly small shows do what is possible to reduce expenses, such as using their own equipment, if they have enough, asking volunteers to help wherever they can, including running an at-cost food stand and, of course, eliminating the show ground rental when the show is on home turf. All this translates into lower entry fees for you. Conversely, rated shows, especially larger ones, cost more to present, and competitors share in those expenses. More classes offered, including specific ones required by the rating carried, mean more of everything else, too, including rings, judges, and ribbons.

However, even at a show as small as what you are probably considering at this point, most instructors will charge a fee for coaching. Figure that it will be about the cost of one of your child's lessons. Particularly with youngsters, this fee covers getting the horse tacked up and your child in the saddle, supervising her in the warm-up ring as she gets herself together and her horse limbered up, and schooling her over a few fences if she will be jumping in any of her upcoming classes. Think of it as a lesson, if you will, but one given at the show instead of at the stable. And the trainer will also soothe your child's fears, bolster her courage, get her into the correct ring at the proper time, and either he or an assistant will remain ringside throughout the class, watching her performance.

If the show is at a stable other than yours, you can count on paying a vanning fee to transport the horse. This cost can fluctuate greatly, but if the show is fairly close by, put down $50, and you should be in the ballpark. If the stable hires a big shipping company, the cost per horse will probably be higher and, if so, it's a bullet you'll just have to bite. Down the road, if your child gets more involved in showing, you can buy a used trailer, maybe in partnership with someone else. Like other costs, vanning fees can be shared if more than one rider will be showing the horse. And while you are tallying up the expense sheet, note that it is pretty common for riders to take a couple extra lessons to iron out little problems and get up to speed before a show.

KEEPING SHOWING EXPENSES DOWN

With an eye to keeping a lid on expenses, remember these tips:

- Show locally—at your own stable, if it runs shows—or at places nearby. It is cheaper to van a horse a few miles than a long distance, and it's cheaper yet not to van at all.

- Unrecognized shows have lower entry fees than recognized ones, and no additional charges for drug testing or not being a member of the USEF or other sanctioning association, which your child probably won't be yet.

- Learn to braid a mane to avoid paying someone else to do it for you. Keep in mind, though, that braiding takes dexterity and time, so, especially when your child first starts doing it, spend lots of time practicing and then allow enough time before a show to get the job done.

- Share a horse when it's feasible. In so doing, you are also sharing rental, vanning, and braiding fees.

How much you want to and can afford to show will be a determining factor in your choice of stable or your later decision to move your child to a different stable. As mentioned in chapter 5, stables with strong reputations as show barns have earned them by putting a major emphasis on training riders for the show ring. They make most of their money from training and from the sale and boarding of horses necessary for this aspect of the sport. Such barns are exciting or daunting, depending on where you and your child are coming from.

While the pressure to show may not be apparent early on when your child is first learning how to ride, you both will feel it eventually at a show barn. At such stables, a substantial number of the riders regularly go to shows. For instructors, having their students "out there" naturally increases their visibility and attracts other riders who, hopefully, see these students doing well. If your child doesn't want to show or you can't afford to let her, in time you may sense that she is getting a little less overall attention, albeit inadvertently, because of this decision. However, if your child wants to show and has your blessing, it only makes good sense to be where the action is.

When Is Your Child Ready for Showing?

By the time your child rides into the show ring, she should be both mentally and physically ready to go. Not only should she be enthusiastic about the idea of going to a show, rather than worried or fearful, but in her riding ability she should be able to hold her own among her peers. She will almost certainly be going with other children from her stable, some of them of her age and riding level, and she should have a chance to bring home a ribbon or two. This does not mean she should go only with the idea of winning. But by being ready, she can comfortably be part of her group, relaxed, and able to enjoy herself.

As she enters the ring, you want her to have a smile on her face, even if in front of an audience it is a little tentative. Riding at a show is not only an athletic endeavor, as riding is anytime, but it's also a performance—a duet between rider and horse, sometimes by themselves, other times in a group. For it to be a positive experience, your child needs to have developed some confidence, poise, and control in her riding. She should be able to think in the saddle and cope if something goes wrong or not as planned.

Your child should be able to do with ease all the things that her instructor asks her to do in a lesson. She should also be able to think clearly and understand and follow directions without getting flustered or panicking.

To be ready to show at all, your child needs to be able, depending on the class, to walk and trot, or walk, trot, and canter around the ring, in both directions, in a group. This means performing each gait when asked and handling her horse in traffic and watching out for other riders. All the while, she should be on the correct diagonal at the trot, which also requires her to recognize whether she is right or wrong and, if necessary, make corrections. Similarly, if her classes require the canter, she must be able to get the correct lead.

If she is going to show over fences, what she is jumping during her lessons ought to be a little more difficult than what she will encounter at the show. Even the simplest course can take on a new dimension with the addition of a flower box in front of each jump or the substitution of low straight rails for crossrails. All the better if what she faces at the show seems easy compared to what she has been doing at home.

Therefore, if your child is still struggling with any of the basic riding skills, if she's still unsure of her diagonals or uncomfortable at the canter and is still worried when asked to jump more than two jumps in a row or her instructor sets up a completely new jump for her to try, it may be better to postpone that first show. By her instructor saying something like, "How about we aim for a show next month sometime?" the tone is kept positive, and she has a goal to work toward.

Chapter Ten

Your Child's First Show

*T*he barn looks different in the early morning, the electric lights more yellow against the dawning sky. But then, this is the first time you have been here at five a.m. You had it in mind to pick up coffee and a donut on the ride over, except your young passenger was insistent that you keep going.

"We don't have time to stop," she said. "The horses have to have breakfast."

"Me, too," you thought wistfully.

You knew from reading the program that the horse show begins at eight a.m. What you didn't find out until last night at dinner, in one of those "Oh, by the way" remarks, was that your child had volunteered to help feed the horses this morning.

Now, you have barely pulled the car to a stop, and she is out the door and gone in a flash. Smiling, you are sure that there has never been such a desire to do chores at home! Although only a few horses are going to the show, your early presence at the barn has awakened all, and they are in unanimous agreement that an early breakfast is a fine idea. No selective feeding here; if one eats, everyone eats! The stomping and snorting make that clear.

It is an appealing time of day, horses stirring, soon contentedly munching on hay and grain. And how impressed you are, watching your child function around the barn as she and the other riders hay, grain, and water the horses quickly yet carefully.

Of course, this is no ordinary day, and the excitement is already building. Each horse going to the show has to have his lower legs wrapped before he can be loaded on the trailer to protect them during the ride. It takes some know-how, and someone with more experience will do this, though you notice your youngster standing by holding leg quilts and wraps.

Yesterday was all about preparation: cleaning and conditioning saddles, girths, and bridles; polishing boots; laundering saddle pads; shampooing horses and braiding their manes. Equipment was gathered together—shanks, extra halters, saddles, saddle pads, girths, bridles, coolers, sweat sheets, fly sheets and fly spray in summer, brushes, rub rags, hoof picks, braiding supplies (in case repairs are called for), water buckets, and whatever else might be needed at the show. But now, with a last-minute check of everything, there is some rushing around for items just remembered.

Your child's riding clothes and gear, what she's not already wearing, is in your car. Probably she's got her breeches and riding shirt on and maybe her boots, but don't forget her hat, hairnets, riding jacket, gloves, and perhaps a crop.

As for you, dressing for comfort around a stable should be second nature by now. But a few extra words about show days. They are *long*, beginning at daybreak and probably capped by more time back at the stable in the evening, putting the horses to bed. The latter is not a requirement, but it's possible your child thinks it is. Anyway, wear comfortable, sturdy shoes; you will be on your feet constantly, for many hours. Over that long a period, temperature and weather can change, so having checked the weather report, be prepared with a raincoat or poncho and an extra jacket or a sweatshirt. And have the same on hand for your child. The extra gear can stay in the car if not needed, but being cold or wet without remedy can ruin the day.

Now all is ready. The early morning chores are done and horses and riders are set to go. The horse transportation—which, depending on how many are going can be anything from a two-horse trailer to a big van—is waiting. One by one the horses, all bathed and braided, walk on like troupers.

Soon you are on your way, with the horse transport in the lead and following right behind, in car after car, the riders and you, their supporters.

What to Expect at the Show

Judging by the number of horse trailers and vans on the road with you, you are headed in the right direction. The instructor had said to follow the stable's van but, best laid plans, you got separated. The presence of these other vehicles is reassuring.

As you turn onto the show grounds, you are met by a sea of cars, trailers, and vans of every make and model, horses being ridden, others being led, still others being lunged, people moving about, and equipment set out everywhere. You find your stable's van and horses, now unloaded and being brushed and tacked up. Your child dashes off to the show secretary's booth with other riders to get the number she will wear on her back.

You stand there, amid all this activity, wondering what you can possibly do to help. If this is all new to you, probably not much more than hold your child's riding jacket, number, and other equipment between classes if asked; be pleasant and encouraging; and walk with your head up, watching where you are going in relation to horses at all times.

GETTING YOUR BEARINGS

At this point, you should take a minute to get your bearings, the better to find your van and others from your stable after you have gone to another part of the grounds. You know how daunting it can be to find your car in a mall parking lot? Well, depending on the size of the show, trying to find your van among row after row of similar-looking rigs can be just as frustrating. Of course, the small show your child will start at won't be too difficult, but getting the lay of the land, particularly the food concession and bathroom facilities, is always a good idea.

Obviously, arrangements are somewhat different if this is an indoor show, mainly in that there are fewer rings with which to contend. Horses and riders will still warm up outdoors, though at some shows they are allowed to do that indoors at designated times between classes. No matter what, vans and horses are parked and tended outside, unless your stable has paid a day rate for stalls for its horses. So, outdoor or indoor show, you will want to get your bearings, whether by locating the various rings or the various doors to the indoor arena.

WARMING UP

If your youngster's first class is early in the program, it is likely that someone else has already tacked up the horse she will be riding. That done, her instructor walks her and her horse down to the warm-up area—sometimes part of a field or, if the stable has enough rings, a ring designated as a warm-up area—gets her in the saddle, fixes the length of her stirrups, and makes sure she's settled. You tag along. "Warm-up?" you say to yourself, "This looks more like a free-for-all." And it frequently does.

Several instructors are standing at different points in the ring, calling commands to their one or two riders, all at the same time. You wonder how your youngster can ever hear her instructor, let alone stay calm in all that traffic!

Riders are going both directions, around the outside rail and across the center of the ring, while others are taking a few jumps, and you are sure you have seen a couple near collisions. Still, miraculously, everyone survives. You may also hear the term *schooling area* or *ring*, but whether it's that or *warm up*, the purpose is to get horse and rider limbered up and thinking about what they are going to do. It is also good training in focusing on what must be done, while coping with the rest, including people watching from the rail and other riders warming up.

The warm-up session will be brief, and in short order you will probably hear something positive like, "Okay, give him a pat." It may not have looked any different to you, but that last bit of riding, whatever it was, must have looked good to the instructor. You remember someone explaining to you that horse and rider should always try to end on a high note.

YOUR CHILD'S FIRST CLASS

After the warm-up session, it is time for your child's first class. Assuming that it will be a flat class, several youngsters will be in the ring at the same time, walking, trotting, and, if called for, cantering on command. If riders from your stable are entering this class, the instructor will be busy making sure everyone is on his or her horse and near the ring's entry gate, ready to walk in. He will do his best to see that everyone is relaxed and ready. It's perfectly okay for you to stand near your child, too, and add a last few words of encouragement.

The ring steward beckons the riders into the ring. They have a chance to walk around for a few minutes, giving both horse and rider a good look at all parts of the ring. Then the steward announces that judging has begun and issues the first instruction: "All walk, please."

You are standing at the rail, feeling both proud and nervous, a hopeful, helpful smile on your face. And while you aren't really sure what is being judged, you think your child looks wonderful. Yes, mistakes occur, and there are differences in ability, but if this is your child's first show, to go into the ring and do what the judge asks is a big first step and a positive experience on which to build. More than that will come later.

Bear in mind that judging is, to some extent (and in some instances, to a great extent) subjective. Certainly, the steward's requests must be met. For example, if the command is to canter, a rider must make her horse canter on the correct lead and not break to a trot until asked to do so. Beyond such basics, the riders all look pretty much the same to you. Suffice to say, this sport takes some watching, in the same way that diving or gymnastics does, before the nuances become apparent. What looks the same initially is, in fact, composed of many shades of gray. Your child's instructor can explain more, giving you a general idea of what a judge is looking for. But not now. Ask him tomorrow, back at the stable.

The Language of Horse Shows

Do take time to savor the sights and sounds you will encounter, not the least of which is the colorful, unique language of horse shows. It crackles over the public address system: "Class eight. Short stirrup riders. Walk, trot, in ring three."

It resonates through the program, with terms such as *schooling break, baby jumpers, puddle jumpers, low hunters, pre-green hunters, pleasure hack,* and *lead line* and abbreviations such as US (under saddle) and WTC (walk, trot, canter).

And the language of shows is in the terse calls of riders in the warm-up ring: "Heads up, vertical. Heads up, oxer." Or the delightfully descriptive critique of a ride that might go: "She dropped his head. She just threw it away." Or, conversely, "Look how well he tracks up, comes right up under himself and engages."

Some things you will figure out like an easy puzzle. Others will leave you scratching your head for a while and will probably be fair game for your youngster's one-upmanship as she tosses out words and phrases, no doubt delighted with her knowledge of a vocabulary you have yet to master. Enjoy it!

Your understanding will grow. Experienced horse people are happy to help newcomers. In addition, the extensive glossary at the end of this book can assist you. Don't feel alone, either. Look around you as you're standing at the rail and, chances are, you will see other perplexed looks. You will recognize them as kindred souls, and your shared confusion will, perhaps, pave the way for a greeting and a shared laugh.

Coping with the Laughter and the Tears

From the moment you arrive at the barn, you can tell the atmosphere is heightened. All the riders, turned out in show attire, exchange greetings as if they haven't seen each other in months. Hairstyles, so often unruly, are now carefully netted, soon to be tucked under a formal riding hat. Your youngster and her friends can be said "to clean up pretty good," in the parlance of stables.

The air crackles with emotions that run the gamut from squeals of delight, to giggles, to quick flashes of temper, to panic at the thought of a forgotten item. It is surely an understatement to say that today is no ordinary day. You wonder how your child will handle all this. It's something you will judge the best. How is she when she has to perform, in the school play, for instance, or when she makes a presentation in front of a group? Does she get nervous, jittery, or wish she didn't have to do it? Or does she handle such situations pretty well? Chances are, something of the same will happen here.

Her instructor can tell you that it's not uncommon for a beginning show rider to go into the ring and promptly forget at least half of what she has learned . . . and only hear half of what is said to her! So, don't be surprised if you see your child, who prides herself on always getting the correct diagonal, blithely begin posting on the wrong diagonal and never even steal a glance to see what she is doing and make the change. Don't start bobbing up and down, trying to tell her through your own body language that she is wrong. Just smile and let it go. The fact that she is in the ring is enough for now.

Like a class trip, a show day is a break in the home stable routine during which riders seem to bond (and band) together, sometimes hardly acknowledging that their parents and other adult well wishers are there at all. Which brings up the question: Should you be there? "Well, of course," you think. "Why shouldn't I?" Yes, chances are you are right, you should be there. Going along to the show is a perfectly fine idea, hopefully even a good and constructive one. Do give it some thought, though. For instance, how does your child react when you watch her lessons (if you do), or even when she just rides by herself? Does she like it, or does she get nervous? Does she ride better when she thinks you are not looking? Think back to when she first started riding (which could equate to a first show now). Was she comfortable with you watching then, or did it take awhile before she got used to it? Or, in fact, has it never been something that worked well for the two of you?

If there's any doubt in your mind, talk it over and try to gauge how your child really feels. If your child would be hurt if you didn't attend, by all means find a way to be there. But if your being

Showing Western Style

Western horses compete at shows as pleasure horses, trail horses, and working cowhorses, with each type of class calling on horse and rider to present themselves in a different manner, performing different tasks, as requested. The smooth, relaxed pleasure horse must behave and move like a perfect, all-day ride.

The trail horse is a confident, unflappable fellow who, at his rider's request, will willingly negotiate a variety of obstacles (bridge, log, or water hazard, allowing the rider to open and close a mailbox, going through a gate and serpentine, and more) and perform maneuvers (including turns on the forehand or haunches, backing, side passes, ground tying, and so forth).

The working cowhorse is an agile, balanced, strong, and otherwise "handy" horse who can show off chores of the traditional ranch horse, such as cutting a calf, team roping, and performing reining patterns. Reining, often called Western dressage, and now an Olympic competition, is also performed in separate competitions. Reining horses show off their agility and precision, acquitting themselves with moves including circle patterns, rollbacks, spins, and sliding stops. Here, as in other Western competitions, American Quarter Horses, Paints, Appaloosas, Arabians, and Morgans are favored breeds.

Competition, to Western riders, means more than formal shows, with kids as young as five preferring the fun of rodeos. Beginning as Little Wranglers, they can show their skills in barrel racing (girls only), pole bending, flag racing, and goat tail untying at Little Britches Rodeos, of which some 250 are held annually in the United States. Little Britches Rodeos are open to contestants up to age eighteen, and high schoolers can also compete in events sanctioned by the National High School Rodeo Association.

there just adds pressure, maybe the best thing for her would be for you drop her off and pick her up at the stable (or even the show grounds) at the end of the day. Or come and go throughout the day, if it's easy to drive on and off the show grounds. At least for the first few shows, this may allow her to work on her riding and confidence level without concerns about you. If you opt for this strategy, though, do be clear about the choice; absence due to indifference is a far cry from a joint decision that a little space will initially be to the good. Be sure, too, that your child is mature enough to stay by herself and that your absence is okay with her instructor.

For most riders, it is a long day, often with long waits between classes. Stable friends, keeping each other company, help pass the time. Also, your child can share in the care and well-being of her horse. Of course, her instructor and his assistant and/or older riders will be sure all are tended to, but bringing a few carrots or taking her horse or another for a short walk to eat grass and relax will be appreciated.

This is like any other all-day outing, so prepare accordingly. No doubt you know the scenario well, from boundless early energy to later-day fatigue and crankiness, and you know what will help the day run smoothly for your child, minimizing any tears or temper that might erupt. Food is always available at shows but, if you prefer, bring your own—a Thermos container of coffee for yourself, perhaps, plus whatever else you would like that is easy to handle. (No barbecues, please.) Plus add to the list nonfood items like a couple of damp face cloths in a plastic bag and, in season, suntan lotion. In all, make it a fun, positive day. If your youngster likes showing, your helpful touches will make it that much more appealing for her to continue.

What to Expect from Your Child's Instructor

At the show, think of your child's instructor as a class-trip chaperone, camp counselor, and cheerleader all rolled into one.

Taking a group of riders to such an event is a big undertaking, and how the day turns out for each individual, and the group as a whole, depends to a great extent on how he organizes and manages things.

If the instructor seems a little less relaxed than he does back at the stable, consider some of what he is responsible for: seeing that all needed horses have arrived at the show looking their best, along with tack and other equipment; making sure that riders know what classes they will ride in; ensuring that horses are tacked up and riders are in the saddle before those classes begin; and a host of other tasks. In brief, much is resting on his shoulders.

With the help of an assistant, if he has one, the instructor will guide your child through the day. How much direct attention he gives her, though, will be determined by how many other riders from the stable are also at the show. Your youngster should, of course, get what attention is reasonably hers, but this is not a day to look for extras.

That said, even if your child's instructor is overseeing several competitors, you can expect him or an assistant to be on hand at key points throughout the day. This is especially true for a beginning rider at her first or one of her first shows. Specifically, he should do the following:

- Get your child on her horse at the appropriate time, warm them both up with a little work in the schooling (warm-up) ring, and then bring them over to the ring where her class is to be held.

- Stay with your child until the class is called and she enters the ring and give her last-minute instructions and encouragement.

- Watch her performance and, afterward, provide a short, positive critique.

After this, very likely, he will be off to help another rider about to go into another class.

Even if you aren't satisfied with the amount of attention your child is getting at the show, be assured that the instructor is doing the best he can. There is hardly a show where problems don't arise. A horse may act up, requiring the instructor to take time to do a little schooling, or one may go lame, forcing a reshuffling of riders to other horses. Another rider may be experiencing particular difficulty and need some extra help. Your child may be getting less attention than others today, but at another show she may be the one getting more. For now, keep your attitude upbeat and any annoyance private.

Remember, your child's instructor is not a babysitter. If your child is very young, you or another adult should plan on being at the show to keep an eye on her. Later on, when she becomes more seasoned, she will probably be able to take care of herself a little more.

What your instructor can do is set a tone that encourages a sense of camaraderie and sportsmanship among his students. Older, more experienced riders can look after their younger counterparts, helping them to feel comfortable at the show. While schooling and critiquing a performance should be handled by the instructor or his assistant, another rider can make sure that your youngster's horse is tacked up with stirrups readjusted (the length may have to be fine-tuned when she gets on) if the saddle has been previously used. Or, if she has her own saddle by now, that must be put on the horse.

Another rider can also see that your child is properly turned out for her class with boots dusted off with a rub rag, hat and jacket brushed, number tied on correctly, and crop in hand, and that she gets to the warm-up ring if her instructor is already there working with another rider. Such a big brother/big sister role can be an enjoyable one for older riders, and it creates a nice feeling of family among all those from your stable.

How You Can Help . . . and Hinder

As your child's parent, the best thing you can do at a show is tune in to her wavelength. She's excited to be there, and you should be, too. It's clearly a milestone to get to her first show and, you suspect, it may well be an event that repeats itself. That being the case, you need to learn how to be a good horse show parent, one who's ready and willing to help, and sensitive as to when to step back.

WHAT YOU SHOULD DO

Quite simply, you can help your child by being supportive, appreciative, and good humored. If you are thinking of doing anything else, such as being negative or complaining, put yourself in the instructor's shoes and take a look at how such behavior appears from his vantage point.

In essence, you should plan on having an enjoyable time at the show. If you do, chances are your child will, too. Your behavior sets an example for good horse show conduct and etiquette, and it helps your child to be the kind of rider others like being around.

Lend a hand where you can, but also know your limitations and only do what you are comfortable doing. If you are able to hold a horse, fine. But if their tendency to dance around, nibble at your hand, rub their forehead on your back, and the like makes you nervous, your hands can just as easily hold inanimate objects such as riding jackets and crops.

It's worth repeating here that as you move around the grounds, you should keep your eyes and ears open and watch where you are going at all times. There are two calls to heed: "Heads up, horse coming through," and, of even greater concern, "Heads up, loose horse." This is, after all, a horse show, and you should conduct yourself as if horses have the right of way, even if they're standing still. If you step out from between trailers without looking and get broad-sided by even a small pony, you are not going to fare so well. Nor do you want to get bumped or kicked because you passed too close to the rump of a fidgeting horse or pony.

And remember to dress comfortably; poor choices, especially in shoes, can make you miserable. The prevailing footing of dirt, gravel, grass, or mud, laced here and there with straw, hay, and bits of manure, calls for a sturdy, closed-toe sports shoe.

Of course, if other family members and friends accompany you and your child, make sure that they, too, understand how to conduct themselves on the show grounds. If small children are included, always keep them in hand and never let them run loose.

Most of all, remember that you are at the show as your child's chief fan and supporter. Be sure to let her know that. During the show isn't the time to fuss at her, before a class reminding her to check her lead or keep her heels down. Just say something about how terrific she looks and how proud you are of her. Or, as trainers like to say to their riders before a class, "Relax and have a good time!"

After the class, if she comes out smiling and holding a ribbon, obviously you will be delighted. But what if she doesn't do so well and comes out of the ring clearly upset? That's when you'll have to contain the situation. It's not a time for much discussion, but instead offer a hug and the reassurance that you know she'll do better the next time. On the drive home, if your child wants to talk about her performance, there'll be time then to listen and maybe offer a thought or two.

WHAT YOU SHOULD NOT DO

You can hinder at a show by trying to run things, even if, as you explain, "It's just my nature." Let your instructor make the decisions now. If you have something to say, be it complaint or constructive criticism, save it unless, of course, it is absolutely critical that he know right away. Be a wise judge of this. In saving your comments, you may come to realize that his way was the right one. If not, at least you will have time to choose your words carefully. Consider this: If you have selected your instructor with care, and if you like what he has done with your child so far, it's a reasonable assumption that he knows how to handle things at a show, too.

Above all, don't coach your child. For all the reasons that it is frowned on at the stable, at a show, add the fact that you will antagonize the judge and maybe even cost your child a ribbon. Even if you are just absolutely sure that a few well-chosen words from you would fix a glaring error or, at least, improve a performance, *don't do it*. If you want to talk about it later at the dinner table, that's up to you. But not when you are ringside.

A constant showing of "expertise" could wind up costing you the instructor who has, in truth, done a good job of teaching your child. Indeed, it's not unheard of that an instructor will finally suggest that you find someone whom you deem more capable. It's too bad if that's not really what you want.

Keep in mind that the objective of this first show is to get your youngster to the horse show, up on her horse and into the ring, through the class, and out again. If this is accomplished and she feels good about herself, you and her instructor have accomplished all you hoped for. When you head home, probably after a stop at the stable to help bed the horses for the night, you should let your child know how proud you are of all she did. Anything else can wait.

Equipment Considerations at This Point: Show Clothes

Since your child began riding, the must-have equipment purchases have been minimal. While there have been options all along, the only items you really had to buy were a riding hat and proper shoes. Now, however, with the decision to compete at horse shows, proper riding attire is required. The price is up to you, but given how quickly kids grow, moderately priced items or secondhand ones might be good choices. If your child continues in the sport, all wearing apparel will have to be replaced anyway.

In all, the riding apparel needed now for English shows consists of a hat, shirt, jacket, breeches, boots, gloves, and a crop. The hat you bought, a regulation riding helmet (ASTM/SEI-certified) with leather chin strap, should be fine. If it is covered in black velveteen or velvet, that is ideal. But other dark colors, notably midnight blue and brown, are acceptable, too. Your youngster may also have gloves, and if they are black or dark brown, you are set. Your child also needs a dark-colored crop. Some kids have neon-colored ones, which undoubtedly get lost far less often around the stable, but they need to stay behind on show days.

The major purchase now will be your child's formal riding jacket—a tailored, fitted jacket of all wool or a wool blend. Your local tack shop will have a selection of them, but if you are sure of her size and there is time both to order it and to return it if the fit is not right, you may prefer to buy from a catalog. (See the sidebar "Tack Suppliers" in chapter 5 for a list of sources.) Again, a dark color is correct; navy blue or black is preferable, but dark green and charcoal gray are also acceptable. The cut of a riding jacket is not the same as that of a blazer or suit jacket, even fitted ones, and they will stand out like a sore thumb if either is worn instead.

As for breeches, again only certain colors are acceptable: beige, light gray, or rust (and white for dressage). You may ride else-where in any color you want, but only the ones mentioned are appropriate for showing. Young children, especially those who are small in size, frequently wear jodhpurs, which are ankle-length breeches with cuffs. These are paired with ankle-high pad-dock boots, again in black or brown, and around the top of the calf, just below the knee, black or brown leather garter straps.

Small children generally look overwhelmed by high, black rid-ing boots. But if all the other riders your child's age are wearing them, it is going to be difficult to convince her not to buy the same thing. If high boots it is, buy black ones (as suggested), off the rack or secondhand. Custom boots cost a small fortune, so at least wait until your youngster's feet stop growing before you invest in them.

High, black rubber boots are an inexpensive option. They don't fit nearly as well as leather ones, but they can be a short-term choice. Ask your instructor's opinion, though. Some think they are okay, and others hate them.

If your child gets leather boots, consider buying her a pair of rubber overshoes, the fold-up kind, to pull on if the show grounds are muddy or just damp from morning dew. Remind her, though, to take them off before she goes into the show ring.

Western Pizzazz

Western show riders are as colorfully and lavishly turned out as their English counterparts are carefully tailored and conservative. Bright colors, satin and embroidery, sequins, and fringe rule the day. But if you are going to take your horse in different types of classes, subtle wardrobe changes are in order.

In pleasure classes, bright colors are acceptable, with shirts and show pants coordinated. Chaps are worn over pants or, if you prefer, jeans. In trail classes, body suits with rhinestones and other glitter are the style.

These are the best ideas for beginners:

- Watch what other riders are wearing at shows, particularly the small changes from class to class.

- If you're on a budget, you can coordinate black or brown chaps with bright tops, saving you the cost of that all-lime or all-red outfit for another time.

- Put what money you can into a good Western hat that will survive wear and tear and hold its shape. Cheap hats won't, and you will just wind up buying another one.

Also, to keep her clean until she rides, have your child pull on a pair of sweatpants over her breeches. Light-colored breeches are magnets for dirt, so have her don the sweatpants before you get to the stable, then take them off just before she gets on her horse.

One last item, another that you are probably buying for the first time, is a riding shirt. Boys probably have one in their wardrobe already: a long-sleeved dress shirt in white or a pastel, worn with a dark tie. Girls, however, need a regular riding shirt with a detachable ratcatcher or choker collar, which, again, can be found in a tack shop or riding catalog. Short sleeves are okay for everyone in hot weather, and girls can even wear sleeveless models. The ratcatcher buttons, invisibly, to the top button of the shirt itself and is usually monogrammed at the throat or worn with a bar pin, plain or with an equestrian motif. Tack shops carry the pins and can have monogramming done.

What brings the picture together and makes it one that judges will notice boils down to being tidy: polished boots (dusted off before each class); clean breeches; clean, neat shirt, especially the front and collar; clean and pressed jacket; and brushed hat. And don't forget: gloves (worn); number tied on, right side up; and crop carried properly. Girls with long hair should wear it pinned up and tucked under their hat. Unless the hair is so short that no wisps poke free, all girls should wear invisible hairnets.

The result for all to see: your beginning rider looking turned out, polished, and in command!

Chapter Eleven

Looking to New Ventures

Not so very long ago you said okay to your child's wish to tackle horseback riding, something you knew little or nothing about. What lies ahead, you wonder? You and your child entered a world that has given you many challenges and good times.

You have gone from finding a stable and an instructor to watching your child become a pretty decent beginning rider, able to hold her own among her peers at the stable. She's taken lessons regularly, learned all about horses, and she's even competed at a few shows.

She's made friends and, in truth, become totally involved in riding. Given the chance, she might actually make her home at the stable! And hopefully, you, too, have made friends, companions standing at the rail, pleased at your children's accomplishments, holding jackets and an occasional horse, and wondering if life will ever be the same again.

This may be the start of a lifelong involvement for your child, a passion that never abates from that first interaction with a horse. Or as with lots of kids, it may last a while, maybe several months, maybe a year or two, and then something else will take its place. Not because your youngster isn't enjoying herself but because the situation changes; friends and school activities bring new interests, the family moves, or for other reasons, this adventure, at least for now, has a foreseeable ending.

Whatever the future, the beauty of horseback riding is that it really can be a sport for people to actively engage in at most any age. Set aside, it's possible to resume it years later, something adults often do. As long as the present experience is good, the door can remain ajar.

In the meantime, how is it working out for you?

"Well, fine," you think. "After all, we're still here."

There's probably no reason to think otherwise, either. Nor are there any hard-and-fast rules for reevaluating what's going on, or actual time lines for doing it. But with the same clear eyes that brought you into the sport, from time to time it's important to take a look at the situation, both in terms of what you've been expecting and, perhaps, what new ideas you may have.

Will Your Child Continue Riding?

Whether your child continues with riding depends largely on her age, how much she has progressed, and how she feels at the moment. Is she pleased with what she's doing but ambitious to do more and more? Or is she pleased, but, at the same time, comfortable with the status quo? Of course, as you know better than anyone else, what she says now could be completely reversed in six months! But it gives you some sense about what or how much, if anything, you may want to change.

First and foremost, is your child still having fun? And right behind that, are you still enjoying yourself? One without the other is a poor mix. Certainly, some kids are focused and achievement oriented beyond what you would normally expect for their age level, but most are still better served when learning and accomplishments are couched in fun, friends, and ongoing encouragement.

You've noticed that your youngster now talks about her "trainer." You're not sure just when that title replaced "instructor," but it seemed to be when she started to feel like she was really riding. A sign of commitment, maybe? And you may have made a change of your own. Nowadays, when you are talking about her, have you caught yourself saying "she rides" as opposed to merely "she takes lessons." And why not? She does have a trainer with whom she rides (as riding parlance would put it)!

You chose this trainer because he taught young children who were beginning to ride. And you continue to like what you see. He is attentive, patient, positive, and good humored, and most times your child comes away from a lesson feeling okay with what happened, even if she wasn't riding well that day, so it sounds like she is in a good spot.

Adding More Learning Opportunities

As your child improves, the natural inclination is to increase her riding education. Her trainer will probably suggest adding a lesson a week or shifting her from group lessons to private or semi-private ones, with an eye toward improving the learning environment. And for sure, as any professional will tell you, lessons are the best way to learn.

As long as your youngster likes the idea and there is time in her week and room in your budget, adding a lesson or otherwise adjusting the lesson plan makes sense. Her schedule, notably keeping up schoolwork and commitments to family and others, is your area to supervise. If adding more lessons to your budget is not an option, you can consider some other possibilities.

One option may be to add some extra riding time outside of lessons. Depending on the stable's lessons schedule and how much the school horses are needed, stables usually let riders rent these horses at reduced rates to use by themselves. When your child has developed some skill and competence, she may enjoy practicing on her own between lessons.

If you haven't seen it yet, check out the fun kids have riding together without an instructor. You may even find yourself standing at the rail with a delighted instructor, watching kids conduct their own informal lesson, as they ride, critique and help each other, and gain a lot from the experience. They can be very inventive, devising exercises for each other or doing a round-robin or follow-the-leader over low crossrails.

Most stables try to help a determined youngster who can't afford the cost of riding. When your child first started, she didn't know enough about horses and stables to take on any chores. But now, with consideration for her age and size, it's very possible that there are things she can do to supplement the cost of at least some lessons or independent riding time.

Adults can sometimes provide in-kind services as well, so if that's your inclination, inquire. Carpenters, painters, graphic artists, those with office skills, to name but a few, may well be able to match skills and needs to the benefit of both parties. Ask what is needed, then make an offer. You never can tell how things will work out.

Riding magazines, books, and videotapes, a selection of which can be found at your local tack shop or in catalogs, can also be useful learning tools. Given that such materials are geared to older riders, much depends on your willingness to watch a video-tape or read an article or a book with your child, discussing ways that the ideas therein could help improve her riding. This type of learning is certainly not on par with actual lessons, but explanations and demonstrations of particular skills or maneuvers could be coupled with independent riding time in which to practice. It's best to be up front with your child's trainer as to your budget limitations and get his support in using some of these teaching aids.

Getting a Solid Foundation

I bet you wish you had a dollar for every time you've heard your child's trainer say, "Flat work, flat work, flat work. It's all about flat work." Even when she started jumping, he kept saying it. It didn't take long to see what he meant, and now even your youngster is appreciating those words.

What he has been talking about is building all the skills that make for good riding technique: balance, a secure seat, proper use of both natural and artificial aids, and, increasingly, being able to get the best performance from both rider and horse. To be sure, this is something everyone works toward. But even at your child's stage, the better she accomplishes this, the better everything flows from it, from a canter around the ring to the approach to a jump.

When your child has mastered the basics of riding, working on technique should become more of a focus. The challenge is to keep

Horses on Radio and TV

If these shows don't play in your area, try calling the contact information or your local stations to see if you can get them added to programming schedules:

The Horse Show with Rick Lamb (radio)
602-279-0900
See www.thehorseshow.com for a list of stations.

Saddle Up Sunday (TV)
Carried on TVG
Dedicated to America's Quarter Horse. Contact the American Quarter Horse Association for more information: 806-376-4811, www.aqha.com.

English and Western programming (TV)
Carried on RFD-TV
See www.horsecity.tv for more information.

it appealing, especially when it can seem to kids that jumping that fence is a lot more exciting than practicing a balanced trot or a trot-canter transition. While both are part of successful jumping, it may not be clear early on just how true that is. In the meantime, continued encouragement and a little bit of peer competition can keep things progressing, and the extent to which your child's trainer can keep flat work interesting and fun will pay dividends.

Regardless of whether your child is riding English or Western, she needs a solid, basic riding education. From this all other things derive. Undoubtedly, by this point, if your child is riding English, she has heard talk of hunters and jumpers, equitation, and dressage. Western riders may become particularly interested in reining or cutting or in one or more rodeo events. Depending on where your child is riding, it may be apparent that, among more advanced riders, most adhere to one discipline or another. Then again, there may be a genuine mix of styles.

Among your youngster's group there's probably conversation about what type of riders they are, or plan on becoming, but the reality of making such decisions is a long way off! In fact, far in the future, if your child ever takes up eventing, she will have to prove herself in three different areas: cross-country over jumps, jumping fences in an arena, and dressage.

At this stage, however, the broader the experience you can offer your child, hopefully combining the rudiments of all disciplines, the better her foundation will be and the better a rider she is likely to become. The disciplines, you will see, interact, and many riders, throughout their riding careers, study and even show in more than one discipline. Horses, too, benefit from the variety.

Of course, not everyone agrees with this. Along the way, you will meet stalwarts who adamantly insist that theirs is the only discipline to follow, and they may even predict dire consequences if you do things other than their way. Hopefully, though, you will meet many more riders and trainers who appreciate how each discipline benefits the other—for example, the value of dressage to hunters, jumpers, and equitation riders and Western riders, and vice versa.

It's important to keep an open mind and encourage your child to do the same. The depth and breadth of the sport, and how many different things you can do, are extraordinary. For kids, learning a little dressage can be just as exciting as taking those first jumps.

Expanding Options: Deciding Where to Go Next

All the hard work is paying off. Your child is now what might be called a seasoned beginner or, as she may like to refer to herself, an advanced beginner. To be sure, she may still be very much a novice, but she has moved ahead and gained a little rank at the stable. There are now some true beginners there, kids who have just learned to turn a horse left and right and move him forward at the walk.

You are delighted with the confidence she has gained, though you're watchful that she keeps things in check. She's a kid, after all, and excited by everything she is learning. It's easy to forget that even the most easygoing, obedient school horse can be a lot to handle if your child asks for more than she means to.

Having mastered the basics of riding on the flat, and having jumped low and inviting versions of several different types of fences, your child is starting to realize how much awaits her. From more shows, to trail rides, to stable time to just rides with friends, to being able to watch advanced riders with an understanding of what they are doing, to trying some different horses herself, your youngster is enjoying the new possibilities.

It could be a good time for you, your child, and her trainer to have a talk about what lies ahead: what she would like to do, what will work for you, and your trainer's ideas regarding some realistic next steps. It doesn't have to be a real game plan, but it's a good idea to check in with each other from time to time and make sure everyone is on the same page. As with any other sport or activity that your child may participate in, she—and you right beside her—can be as involved as you want.

Certainly, if she has enjoyed her initial exposure to showing, there can be more of the same. Just about anywhere you live in the country, there are shows to go to, many of which are held year after year at the same stables. It's fun to listen to your newly experienced rider and her friends talk knowingly about the various shows and where they want to go next season. Soon enough you, too, will have your favorites: shows that are managed better than others, or where the setup is more hospitable to the riders, the food is tastier, or there are some wonderful shade trees for when you've had your fill of sun.

For the future, you will need to consider a couple things: Does this trainer train older children and more advanced riders, or are beginning riders his specialty? If the latter, you will have to switch to another trainer at some point. Also, how do all his riders do at shows? Compared to riders from other stables, are they well schooled and well turned out?

While going to shows to win is not something to think a lot about at this point, never bringing home a nice ribbon can be a warning sign. It's rarely the fault of the rider or the trainer alone, and the combination of the two should be able to produce some ribbon-worthy trips around the ring.

You didn't raise any concerns at the shows, especially as you knew that with the first show, or first few shows, just getting your child on her horse, into the ring, through the class, and back out again was all that was hoped for. But now, having had time to assess the situation, maybe you have some questions. Or, going forward, perhaps there are things you can do, albeit as an interested bystander, to help improve things.

With thoughts of more shows, the question of budget may come up again because if your youngster enjoys going to shows and does well at them, they can become very appealing events. Before you notice, they can also become a pretty expensive item. If it matters, a little planning as to how many shows you can afford and how frequently can avoid disappointment later, especially when that could mean missing a particularly popular show that just about everyone else is going to.

Even shows that your child is not going to—either a local show or one that's well known and within a reasonable distance—can be worth dropping in on just to watch some classes. Try some different ones, if you can, such as hunter-jumper competitions, dressage shows, or whatever else is around that strikes your fancy. Whatever the discipline, it can be both a lesson and an inspiration for your child to see more advanced riders compete. And don't just watch the formal classes, either. Stand at the rail of the warm-up ring for a while and see what riders do to prepare themselves and their horses.

You should encourage your child to do the same at shows where she is competing. Watching other riders can be a relaxing break before her next class, even as it plants some useful ideas. How do other riders conduct themselves? How do various ones ride a course? What riders look especially sharp? Is it their clothes and, if so, what about them? How is their horse turned out? Maybe you will stand at the rail with her, maybe she will hang out with her friends. Either way, there is a lot to see and talk about.

Finally, this is a good time to give the stable a review. Do you still feel comfortable there? Is your child, with you supporting her, so enthused about showing that a real show barn might be in your future? After all, if youngsters your child's age are going to lots of shows, the enthusiasm can be very stimulating. It's important not to make a change without some thought, though. Your child's trainer may be happy to go to more shows if he just knows there's more interest.

Now that you have been exposed to riding for a period, are there things about your stable's facilities that you wish were different, maybe nothing you would make a change for yet, but perhaps food for thought a little later? Do you wish your stable had an indoor arena? Would you like to see a few more school horses, so that youngsters like yours could have some different riding experiences?

About this point, however, you need to be cautious in your criticism. If there are not enough school horses for the number of beginning riders, that may certainly be a problem. But if you think the available horses can't provide enough challenge as riders progress, you may be very surprised. With a better rider on his back, that laid-back school horse will probably exhibit a lot more sparkle than you imagined. And as your rider improves her techniques, she, too, will find that this same horse has a lot more depth than she knew. Or, as she may remark, "It's amazing how good he is getting!"

The "Horse of My Own" Bug

It's likely to happen . . . your youngster may start to say things that sound suspiciously like she is thinking about having a horse of her own. You aren't especially surprised. Certainly, it's nothing like that long-ago (or so it seems) time when she announced that she wanted to learn how to ride. That was a real shocker.

After all, you both have been spending a great deal of time at a stable, the primary function of which is to board horses—that is, privately owned horses. So the notion of ownership is all around. There are adult owners and, undoubtedly, some teenagers, too. But how badly your child wants a horse of her own will probably depend more on who in her age group at the stable becomes an owner. If a couple of them get horses, the idea will surely blossom for others, including, no doubt, your child. She sees it as such a natural next step, particularly if, in her mind, there can be no life without horses.

This belief may be coupled with quite a forceful campaign. How it unfolds will have her imprint all over it. Her schoolwork may improve, as may her spirit of helpfulness around the house; the word *horse* may appear on any and all gift lists; and your child may even draw up a proposal for keeping her horse, including a floor plan of where he could stay, if keeping him at home is even an option. She may make financial efforts, too, including saving her allowance and doing any extra chores that will raise cash.

As beguiling as all this is, unless, as has been the case all along, money is no object, saying something to at least slow the process can buy time. "Whoa" is good.

Unless you are absolutely sure that a horse, once purchased, will find a secure place in your family—other siblings will ride him or, perhaps, you yourself will—look before you leap. It is good advice for anyone, no matter how sure they are about wanting a horse. It is even more prudent for you and your child who, no matter what she promises, may be on to the next great passion a year from now, at which point you will be disentangling yourself from horse ownership.

On the flip side, it's far better that you both understand what is involved by getting your toes wet in any of several other arrangements. Buying a horse outright, only to find out that it is more than you can handle, can be heartbreaking for all concerned, especially when you have to tell your child that she won't be able to keep the horse with whom she has now fallen totally in love.

But no matter what, for your child any horse, purchased or otherwise, must be completely suitable. You are looking for a horse every ounce as trustworthy as one of the school horses she has been riding. Another term you may hear is *packer*, which is a horse that will pack your kid around. Ask your trainer's help in finding one. He will choose a horse with whom your child can ride and learn. If you can't find something, be patient. The horse business is very fluid, and one will turn up.

Meanwhile, your child is continuing to ride and improve, which speaks to the wisdom of a semipermanent arrangement at this stage for another reason: It also allows her to gain experience on a few horses without the complication and financial outlay of buying and selling.

Be open to the possibilities and choose what feels like it will work best for your child and the rest of your family. Whatever the arrangement, it's important to go in with your eyes open and find out as much as you can. You will soon know whether owning a horse is something you and your child are still game to pursue.

LEASING AND CO-LEASING

As for trying life with a horse on a semipermanent basis, you should first consider leasing or co-leasing one. This, in a sense, is a long-term rental, usually for six months or a year. You need to try to get some background on your prospect in terms of his general health and so forth.

While there is no initial investment with a lease, during the lease you are responsible for regular expenses, all of which should be spelled out in a written agreement. You should expect the lease fee to include the monthly board, but will it also include all veterinarian and farrier bills? Do you take care of everything, or just reasonable expenses? Twice-yearly shots, periodic wormings, floating teeth, and minor health problems are one thing, but if the horse gets seriously ill or injured, who will pay for the treatment? That can get very expensive. Similarly, a horse who requires corrective shoes can run up your farrier costs. Will the owner absorb costs over a certain level, or will you pay for everything?

Be sure to ask, as well, who is responsible if the horse suffers serious loss of use or dies. It's not pleasant to think about, but as you can imagine, any such occurrence can turn a workable arrangement into something far from appealing. You should also find out how much notice you will receive in the event that the horse is sold.

Co-leasing is another possibility. In this case, a written agreement is essential, and all the same questions need to be settled. But overall, if there are two parties, you can expect everything to be half that of a full lease: half the responsibility and expense, but also half as much time with the horse. Some of the horse's "belongings" may be made available to you, such as blankets, leg wraps, and grooming supplies, but you will want your own saddle and bridle. It's also possible that the owner will want your child to have most or all of her own equipment, rather than risk the owner's things getting worn out or lost.

Co-leasing can be a good sharing experience for your child or a difficult one, and you will be the best judge of that. In general, how is she about sharing her things? How has she been when others have ridden her favorite school horse, the one she almost always has for her lessons? Remember the day she was expecting to ride him, but you got to the barn late and another beginning rider was already tacking him up?

Because this arrangement is for children, adults are also involved. You will have to work out who rides when and how flexible each party can be. If the horse can be taken off the premises, will the youngsters share him at a show or plan on going to different shows? You'll have to decide many such things. The benefit of leasing, whether you hold a full lease or a co-lease, is that if the situation doesn't work out for some reason, you can look for another horse when the lease is up.

INFORMAL ARRANGEMENTS

Instead of formally leasing or co-leasing a horse at this point, you may find an informal arrangement that works for all. Perhaps a friend would be willing to let you bring his backyard horse to your stable, picking up agreed-on costs and taking things month to month without a lease. Or a boarder at your stable may offer to let your child frequently ride her horse—one absolutely suited to your child, of course—with a "let's see how it goes" attitude. Maybe the other rider is too busy to ride much, and while some money may change hands, it is more important that someone is available to give the horse a lot of love and attention, as well as some exercise.

Chapter Twelve

Buying a Horse for Your Child

*Y*ou may not be to the point of saying that the idea of buying a horse has passed muster, but you are willing to seriously talk about it. That says that you have batted the pros and cons back and forth. And even if your child is totally convinced that owning a horse is the most wonderful idea in the world, you prevailed and tried out a less permanent arrangement first.

You're reasonably certain that your youngster is going to stay with riding, at least for the foreseeable future. Young as she is, you have been quite impressed with how she's managing the various parts of her life and demands on her time. She keeps up her schoolwork, she still sees all her nonriding friends, and she spends lots of time with the rest of the family, even though she tries to get everyone to spend more of it at the stable.

Perhaps you have tried leasing a horse, with the happy result of coming through this prepurchase "test" with flying colors. Simply put, your child, and you, as well, had a wonderful time taking care of and being responsible for a horse. Yes, believe it or not, you went to the stable even more than you had before, and you wanted to go, in fact. Though you weren't actually owners, in a sense you were coming to see *your* horse.

Before you jump into ownership, you need to carefully go over the projected costs (discussed later in this chapter) and make sure the family budget can handle it. Owning a horse can be an extra-ordinary experience, but—it bears repeating—also an expensive one. If finances are a worry, having a horse will wind up being a lot less fun.

If you're not sure, you should wait awhile. Unraveling owner-ship takes time and money, and it brings disappointment. You need to be confident of this next move yourself, even if your youngster is impatient.

What about Co-Owning?

A horse of her own is your child's dream. But no matter how you crunch the numbers, it just isn't going to work out. But everything else seems right—her dedication and willingness to make time for her own horse—so you hate to give up the idea completely.

You've had talks with her trainer and he agrees, if it can be worked out, it's a good time for her to have her own horse. He has had enough experience with youngsters to know when the time is right and, also, when it's too soon, and you trust his judgment. Then one day he offers a solution: If the right partners were inter-ested, what would you think about co-owning a horse? Maybe he knows of a horse that he wishes one or more of his riders could have.

It's food for thought and certainly a possible way to take the next step. But what about sharing? Would it be trickier with chil-dren or, if the parents lay the groundwork, could it be a good learning experience? As with other things, much depends on how you think your child will react. If it's the only way to own a horse at this time, will all concerned make it work? (If you have already had a successful co-leasing arrangement, essentially these ques-tions have been answered in the positive. Your youngster has proved herself to be a good partner, capable of sharing, and con-siderate of the other child involved, which should give you confi-dence moving forward.

If your trainer has had experience setting up a co-ownership between families with young beginning riders, ask for his help.

Maybe there is another child at the stable whose family is in the same situation. For starters, the adults should see if both sides are comfortable with the idea. Besides the obvious financial benefits, having two kids equally committed to the well-being of their horse, and covering for each other during family vacations, illness, schoolwork overload, and the like, could be very appealing. Are the two riders of similar ability? If there is an appreciable difference, a horse can develop bad habits from the lesser rider, which is a potential frustration for the better rider.

As with any partnership, it's important to take the time to listen to everyone's questions and concerns and to hammer out all the what's and what if's. You need to put everything in writing and make sure both parties have copies. How will the youngsters handle their lessons, independent riding time, and shows? Will they take lessons together, alternating who rides their horse and who rides a school horse (which is a good way to keep riding different horses)? Will they come to the stable at different times, or will they meet at the stable and share the riding between lessons? Will there be enough different classes for them to enter at shows? And finally, you need to consider what will happen if one party wants out of the arrangement. How will that be handled, and how much notice is expected?

If two savvy youngsters put the focus on their horse, united in what is best for him, co-owning could work out beautifully. And who knows? When these kids outgrow this first horse, maybe they will opt to share the next one.

It's Not the Purchase Price, It's the Upkeep

As you pursue the idea of buying your first horse, you take comments about upkeep being far more than the purchase price on other people's say-so, plus what you have observed. After you have become an owner, you know it for an absolute fact. The costs—stabling, horse gear, vet bills, farrier—are "always something" and never ending. The money for even a good beginning horse, which for a child will actually be a pony or small horse that is likely to be pricey, is only the start of what you'll be laying out. Remember that you'll still be paying for tack, lessons, riding gear, and shows; you will begin to appreciate what's in store.

It's important to keep your eyes open about costs and not pretend you know better than everyone else and "can work it out." Broke but happy may be a horse person's natural state, but that's after the bills are paid.

VET AND FARRIER SERVICES

To be sure, there's a price range for just about every item. Only veterinarian and farrier fees are pretty much the same within an area, relating only to services or products provided. Some stables would rather you use the same vets and farriers that management uses, and at other places you can use who you want.

With both veterinarian and farrier fees, question bargain prices. If you find someone who is way off the mark, it could be that he is new to the area and trying to establish himself, or it could be that he is not very good. Be wary. You may be able to save elsewhere, but not on your horse's health or his feet!

Most vets will work out a payment schedule with you if you get hit with a sizable bill, which can happen. It will be wonderful if spring and fall shots plus periodic wormings are the sum of your yearly vet bills, but it's the incredibly lucky owner (does one exist?) whose horse doesn't go lame at one time or another or for some other reason require extra visits from the vet. As for the farrier, you pay according to the type of shoes your horse requires, per shoeing session, which, on average, is about every six weeks.

MONTHLY BOARD

Of the other costs, monthly board will be your biggest item. If you like the stable you are at and the price is right, you are all set. Your child's trainer is there, as are her friends, and you are both familiar with the way the stable operates. If you need to house your horse somewhere else, do some shopping around. Of course, if you plan on co-owning your horse *and* stabling elsewhere, that will mean both riders have to move to a new stable, which can get complicated.

Call around for prices and then stop in at various stables, much as you did when you were looking for a place for your child's lessons. Now, though, you go with a more practiced eye, having spent a good bit of time around barns, yours and others. Also make a point to talk to boarders. The latter will add their personal views—some good, some bad—to the basic facts but, overall, they will help you get a more rounded picture. No stable pleases everyone all the time, but you do want to feel comfortable at yours. It is, after all, just about your second home.

Boarding stables provide various levels of service:

- **Full-service stables:** These stables, quite literally, do everything for you and your horse, from grooming your horse and cleaning your tack, to having your horse tacked up when you arrive to ride. After you finish riding your horse, stable staff untack, bathe, walk out, and put him back in his stall.

- **Full-board stables:** These stables provide your horse with grain, hay, and water; a clean stall daily; and turnout. Staff also keep watch over your horse, monitoring his health and well-being. For you and your child, both new to the sport, this is probably the most practical choice—providing good basic care for your horse, yet leaving you lots of room to participate and learn.

- **Partial-board stables:** At these stables, bedding is provided for your use but you are expected to clean your own stall. Management feeds, hays, and waters your horse, but turnout and the rest of his care are left to you.

Again, prices vary, not just between basic types of stables but also within a category, where more and better facilities drive up the price. How important is it to you that the stable have an indoor arena, a separate dressage ring, or a fancy jumping ring?

To Insure or Not to Insure

Whether you insure your horse is up to you. Some people insure for both full mortality (death) and major medical, others only for the latter. Some insure an expensive horse, but not a cheaper one. Others base their decision on completely different criteria. Talk with some horse owners at your stable, both those who have insured their horses and those who have not, and listen to what they have to say.

The following insurers can give you a place to start and will be happy to discuss the question of insuring your horse:

Broadstone Equine Insurance Agency
888-687-8555
www.broadstonequine.com

Horse Insurance Specialists, Inc.
800-346-3271
www.horse-insurance.com

Kaplow Insurance Agency
800-623-0201
www.kaplowinsurance.com

Nichols Farms Insurance (The Hartford Group)
812-359-4108
nfci@speedex.net

These are but a few of the many companies insuring horses. Others advertise in horse magazines and online, among other places.

And what extras will you pay for? Some stables provide the same feed ration to all horses and charge if yours needs more to eat. Other stables figure small appetites and big appetites even things out naturally and charge the same for all. You should also expect to tip stable staff if you need your horse turned out more than usual, and for other extras.

TACK

Chances are your youngster has been collecting grooming supplies, bits and other tack items, and perhaps more riding clothes, too. But now you need to outfit your child's horse with an anti-sweat sheet, a cooler, and, come winter, a good, warm blanket. Plus you need leg wraps, first aid supplies, and lots more. Your child will pour over the myriad selections in catalogs and at Web sites, choosing the perfect items for her horse.

The good news is that this is an area where you have some latitude. You can pay top dollar for the finest equipment, or you can buy things that are every bit as attractive and serviceable at budget prices. Either way, a horse can be just as well cared for. For example, there are plenty of modestly priced blankets that will keep your horse just as warm as fancier models. And if you or someone you know is adept with a sewing machine, fleece liners and other modifications are not hard to come by. As well, don't forget about eBay. You can find almost anything you want there, from apparel (for her and her horse) to tack. Check in "sporting goods," then "equestrian," or just search for the items you're looking for. (See chapter 5 for a list of tack suppliers, plus other money-saving tips.)

LESSONS AND SHOWS

The last costs you will want to factor in are your child's lessons and shows. How much you spend on both is up to you, but part of your youngster's excitement in owning a horse will be in learning to ride him well and taking him to shows.

Especially with a new horse, it's quite understandable that she and her trainer will think some extra lessons can help in getting horse and rider acclimated to each other. It may also be necessary for your trainer to give the horse some schooling sessions, which amounts to riding and training the horse himself, so that he is easier for your child to ride. Your trainer will charge for these, too, but less than for a lesson. Bear in mind, this is a special time, and starting out the best way possible is very important.

Involving Your Trainer

You want your child's thrill at riding to continue and not soon evaporate in favor of something new. Being more concerned than she is when it comes to her horse's need for exercise is not a position you want to be in too often. It is also important for your child to develop enough confidence and ability so that she can actually *ride* this horse. As much as he must be a solid and trustworthy citizen, he should have enough ability to help your child improve as a rider.

You can form a really good partnership—you, who knows your child best of all, and her trainer, who has had the experience of teaching many youngsters to ride. He has a good sense of the right time to buy your youngster her first horse and when it's too soon.

As you sort through the process, you need to keep your trainer involved. After all, he will be training both your child and her horse. He's a professional, and you can count on him to see things and ask questions that don't occur to you. He has a good idea what type of horse will make a good match for her. Whether it is a Connemara pony, small Quarter Horse, Morgan, Arabian, Thoroughbred, or other breed, or a grade horse is far less important than that the horse be absolutely suitable for your child. With the help of your trainer, you can be sure to get a suitable horse. Don't settle for anything less.

Your youngster will probably fall in love with every horse that looms as a possibility, and there may be tears when it is not "the one," but be as tough minded as you can be. You can always find a horse to love. As many times as you need to, say to your child and yourself, "There will be another one, another day. Be patient."

Many trainers teach lessons at more than one stable and know of specific horses for sale, or they may be able to direct you to likely sources. A horse could even come into your stable on speculation. It may be that you do the early scouting, then ask the trainer to look at any horse that strikes you as a good possibility. He will probably ride the horse or, if it is too small for him, have an assistant or advanced rider do it in his presence. If that goes well, then your child will take her turn.

159

Many trainers charge for their assistance in negotiating a deal. You can arrange this with yours, either paying him per horse he looks at or a percentage (10 percent is common) of the purchase price of the horse you decide on. As to that price, as with many a major purchase, the reality is that you will probably pay a little more than you planned. If so, you should live with it, not moan and groan. Once your child has her horse, she will have the time of her young life!

What Makes a Good First Horse?

Your child's first horse should have the soul of one of the school horses she has been riding. Maybe he'll be a little fancier looking, if she intends to do much showing, but in experience and temperament he should be like one of the "schoolies." You should stick to that blueprint and not let your child get overmounted. And no green horses—that is, beginning horses—for a beginning rider.

You will also hear the good-as-gold horse you want called a school master or packer, the latter for a horse that will pack your kid around a course. The horse you are looking for will probably be older—"have some age on him," it will be said. He's a made horse, steady and dependable. As you watch him through the ensuing months, you'll be convinced he's getting so much better as your child's riding improves. The truth is, just like those school horses, he knew these things all along. He was just waiting for your youngster to learn how to ask for something, and then he delivered.

So how do you find such a horse? Besides whatever suggestions your trainer can offer, you can check the classified ads in your local newspaper, keep watch over stable bulletin boards, and tell friends and associates what you are looking for. If you and your child are checking around before involving your trainer, and you find a horse you like, ask if the horse's owner will ride him for you. You will see what the horse is capable of, ridden by someone who knows him well. Keep your eyes and ears open at shows, too, because that's another good place to see a "for sale" horse under tack.

In looking for a horse for a beginning child rider, you won't see the choices you would if you were in the market for a horse for a more advanced, older rider. Less choice also means less variation in the selection. Your child's size will also dictate whether it needs to be a small horse, a pony, or even a small pony. Though the latter will be outgrown faster, good ponies are expensive. Nonetheless, if your child does well with him, he should carry a good resale value.

Finally, you should try to find out why the horse is being sold. "Sadly outgrown" is a common reason, and it's okay as long as it is because the rider outgrew him in size. That the animal's wicked personality has worn out its welcome is a less acceptable one. If the family is moving, ask why they're not taking the horse. Whatever the reason for selling, dig a little and ask questions.

Vetting before You Buy

You should get a full examination of the horse you buy (often called vetting out) before any money changes hands. This exam should be conducted by an impartial, third-party veterinarian, one who does not normally take care of the horse in question. The reason, of course, is that you don't want his opinions swayed by prior affiliation. Besides judging the horse's health and well-being, the vet will evaluate his serviceability for what your child, her trainer, and you want him to be able to do.

The first thing the vet will ask you and your child is, "What do you want to do with him?" As enthusiastic as your child is, she will probably not be too clear in her answer, "I don't know. A little bit of everything, I guess," is pretty typical—and why your trainer's guidance will be helpful.

You have already agreed that what your youngster needs is a small horse or pony who is safe, has a kind disposition, and is well schooled. Also, he needs to be a decent mover, a capable jumper, and versatile enough to help her improve. To find all these attributes in one animal is enough of an order. Don't add unnecessary features to the shopping list. It will be another horse, another day who will be the one to jump big fences and win regional or national honors. That will be horse number whatever, some years from now.

Vetting is a long exam, and because of the amount of time required, it's more expensive than a usual vet visit. It is also essential to do. Especially if you don't know the horse, it will give you a detailed picture and maybe point out something that will cause you to nix the deal or maybe just tell you things that can help in managing the horse now and in the future. And even if you know the animal and someone suggests that you needn't bother to vet him, do it anyway. When someone wants to sell a horse, it's surprising what he or she can "forget" to tell you. It may well be something with which you can easily live, but that is for you to know first, before you buy.

It's your choice as to who vets this horse. Don't be pressured to use anyone else's recommendation, such as your trainer's, unless you are comfortable with it. By now you are familiar with some of the veterinarians who work on horses at your stable, and it is perfectly okay for you to approach one of them yourself. Remember, as much as you want this horse, you want him to pass (or fail) on the facts, and not for any other reason. You should use a vet you respect and listen to him. He will collect his fee whether you buy the horse or not.

Much of the exam is set, but some parts (including x-rays and laboratory tests) are optional. The vet may feel that certain tests and x-rays are worthwhile to do, and they may be, but they will also increase the cost of the exam. If in the course of the exam it becomes clear that the horse will not be serviceable for your needs, most veterinarians will not proceed, thus saving you the full cost and time.

In brief, the exam involves a full going-over of the standing horse at rest, looking at conformation and the health of all parts. The vet will also examine him in motion, at the walk, trot, and canter, first without tack, then ridden, and again after exercise. With the seller's permission, the horse's regular vet can furnish the examining vet with information regarding the animal's health history.

Experienced vets can usually tell if a horse is drugged, so be sure to ask if the horse you're considering appears to be drugged. If the word on the street is that drugging goes on at a particular stable, or it's even alleged that it does, you shouldn't buy a horse from there. Especially when it's going to be a child's horse, you don't want lameness problems that were camouflaged or a snappish personality that was damped down by "a little something" while you and your youngster were around. No rider does, but with kids, it's doubly bad news.

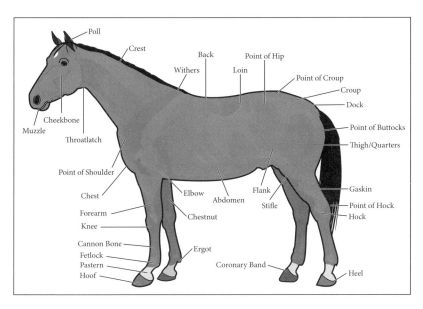

The parts of a horse.

The veterinarian who will vet the horse you want to buy will give you his professional evaluation, as well as his considered opinions about this animal. What he can't do is make up your mind for you. By now, you and your child have gotten to know the horse a little, visiting his stable or having him shipped to your place. Hopefully, your child has ridden him in a lesson, and by herself, and handled him on the ground. You have also checked to see if he has any stall habits that could be a problem. So you probably have some gut reactions.

Absolutely, you should talk with people whose opinion you respect, as they may be able to put to rest any uncertainty you have. But despite this, if something doesn't sit right with you, don't waste your money and everyone's time vetting the horse.

Trying Out a Horse

If you want to take the horse for a trial period, if the owner allows it, you can have the horse shipped to your stable and let your child ride him several times over a week or so. It's a good thing to do in any case, but if you have any undue concerns, it's a must. Alternately, if you can't have him brought to your stable, see if your child can ride him where he is. In this case, you should arrive unannounced with saddle and tack in hand, several times, at different times of the day. If anyone questions you, be polite and vague, but don't yield on these drop-in visits. If the horse's personality changes, or if he starts to exhibit unsoundness, that's a red flag. You can listen to all the explanations given, but something is amiss, and you should keep looking.

True, your child will be at a stable with lots of other people who potentially can give her a hand, but there are sure to be times when she will be there with very few others. She must be totally at ease with her horse—picking up his feet and otherwise working around him, tacking up safely, and, of course, riding. It sounds so basic, but to be afraid of your horse is no fun.

Life with a Horse in the Family

Is it possible that your child will want to spend more time at the stable than she does already? Yes is the resounding, albeit simple, answer. There is nothing like the power of "my horse" to make increased time a must. You better get used to it or, at least, resign yourself. Warn the rest of the family that there will be more late dinners. There will also be a great deal of fun, plus the endless delight in watching your child totally enthralled with her new horse.

Your child's horse is a member of the family, a big one, need it be said, both literally and figuratively. He will take center stage

Pony Club

Much awaits your child as she and her horse grow together, learning and experiencing many different activities. One that could be just the ticket for youngsters with more energy and ambition than money is joining a chapter of Pony Club. This junior equestrian organization puts the emphasis on developing horsemanship and team spirit, and it offers education and competitions in dressage, combined training, show jumping, games, polo, polocrosse, fox hunting, and more.

With more than 12,000 members and 600 chapters across the country, there is very likely a group in your vicinity. Or, you and other interested adults can start your own. In fact, the U.S. Pony Club counts on adult participation to keep its clubs viable. Sound interesting? Check out the organization's Web site, www.ponyclub.org, for some terrifically readable and encouraging guidelines that just might get you thinking about becoming involved.

Most Pony Clubbers have their own horses, though membership is also open to nonowners who have access to horses. Some clubs may be able to arrange lease or borrowing arrangements. Members carry rankings and work their way up a nine-step rating program through tests, from D to A, demonstrating skills in riding and ground work. Dues are kept moderate, and the only stated equipment requirements are an ASTM/SEI-certified riding helmet, leather shoes or boots with heels, and suitable clothing. As the organization likes to point out, custom boots don't matter, but keeping whatever you own clean and polished does!

before you know it! If you thought you were involved before, now you are responsible for a horse. He is your child's—and yours.

Of course, the stable staff will see that he is okay. You are paying for that. But they are responsible for the care of all the stable's horses every day, so even if they want to, they cannot give too much attention to any one horse. You will see both your child and her horse blossom as, through love and attention, they develop a special bond.

Pony Club, trail rides, stable lessons, and local shows are just some of the many activities your child will enjoy with a horse. Much is involved and much is possible through horse ownership. Whether or not it is for your child and you now, or sometime in the future, is a very individual and complex decision. But if you have given yourselves the green light to take that step, tally ho!

Chapter Thirteen

Riding— A Family Affair

*N*o doubt, we have a rider in the family," you delightedly think to yourself, a proud parent of your accomplished youngster.

From the day she first set things in motion, startling you with "Can I learn to ride?" she has come so far. Just look at her now: happy, involved, learning more all the time, and making her way in this exciting sport.

The truth is, you have both come a long way. Indeed, whether you have grown to love the sport as she does or your comfort zone is a little more reserved, you have learned to negotiate uncharted waters. And you have lived to tell the story!

It has brought you to the end of this book, but quite possibly the beginning of many more years of horseback riding somewhere in your life. It could well be that your youngster continues in the sport—improving and trying new challenges—to a more competitive level of showing, other disciplines, and perhaps someday a high school or college equestrian team.

You must admit that as you watch her riding her horse, you've found yourself intrigued. Could it be that you would like to try to ride, too?

"Oh, no," you say to yourself. "Not me. I'm too, too . . ."

Too what? Is it possible that having participated in your child's experience, you can now view the sport of horseback riding with far less trepidation, even to thoughts of getting on a horse yourself? And why not? Riding is for all ages, whether you begin as a child and continue in it or don't pick it up until adulthood. Nudged by your youngster's involvement, you just might try it now for the first time! There are even cases where a parent and child start riding lessons together, and the child soon moves on to another interest, leaving the parent totally captivated and committed to riding.

You won't be the same kind of rider your child is. She's a natural learner. After all, that's pretty much what kids do—listen to other people and learn from them. She's naturally balanced, too. The years haven't knocked her body this way and that. And at her young age, she's blissfully unaware of her own mortality.

You, in contrast, bring intellect to the sport; that is, you are able to think critically and understand. You are also probably more cautious than you used to be, having lived through some spills and injuries, minor though they hopefully were. And even if you are braver than most, it is a rare adult who is totally fearless.

What's important to remember is how many levels of riding are open to you, depending on what you hope to achieve. There is no right way, only your desire to give riding a try. Your youngster did. Why not you?

And what about other family members? Seeing one child having such fun can persuade siblings to try. And families can make riding a great "togetherness" sport. Think what fun a weekend trail ride can be or even a vacation at a dude ranch! Just about anywhere you live or travel, some form of horseback riding is likely to be available.

Perhaps riding is something you've always wanted to try. Or something you've wanted to do again. Or a brand new idea. Whatever your starting point, you will almost certainly meet your counterparts. From your child's age or younger to well on in life, the sport can be a wonderful adventure for anyone willing to throw a leg over a saddle.

Maybe you will revisit childhood dreams of learning to ride, going to shows, and winning ribbons. Or maybe you will just revel in the companionship of a gentle horse, still capable of giving you an energetic walk, trot, and canter when you ask properly. However the sport invites you, you, too, will discover that horseback riding is an extraordinary experience.

Appendix

Therapeutic Riding Programs

From that first sighting, when a youngster's eyes lock onto these beautiful, strong, and athletic creatures, who can argue with the power of horses to be a force for change? They teach, challenge, heal, direct, and encourage in so many ways.

What isn't so apparent is that it doesn't stop with the kids who learn to ride at their neighborhood stable. Indeed, the reach of horses goes far beyond what most people would imagine. An extraordinary group of these animals, stars of therapeutic riding centers across the country, are helping individuals with physical and mental disabilities to accomplish what they might never have thought possible: to horseback ride. And while it is important to note that people of all ages can be helped, from very young to late in life, at most centers you'll find that children and adolescents are the largest group involved in therapeutic riding.

If you have a child with special needs, have you ever imagined that horseback riding might be something she could do? Perhaps it's something about which you have already thought. But if not, this wonderfully designed approach to riding might be worth a serious look.

There could be several opening scenarios. Your child may surprise you, as many of them will do, by asking if she can learn how to ride. Or maybe it will be subtler, as she wonders aloud if she will ever be able to do such a thing. Then again, depending on the situation, it may be up to you to take the initiative and decide, with expert guidance, that therapeutic riding is something to pursue.

What Can Be Achieved?

Therapeutic riding is a term that covers an extremely diverse group of programs that benefit just as wide a spectrum of youngsters with physical, cognitive, psychosocial, and emotional problems. According to the North American Riding for the Handicapped Association (NARHA), which is the national organization most closely involved with the movement, children with the following disabilities are commonly involved in therapeutic riding: muscular dystrophy, cerebral palsy, visual impairment, Down Syndrome, mental retardation, autism, multiple sclerosis, spina bifida, emotional disabilities, brain injuries, spinal cord injuries, amputations, learning disabilities, attention deficit disorder, deafness, and stroke.

At the center of a complex activity, the horse becomes the great equalizer. Whether a child uses a wheelchair or walks with crutches, has low self-esteem or a poor self-image, she can attempt to ride a horse. Most often done in a group setting, therapeutic riding can be used in several key ways.

For some children, it is recreation, offering the same opportunity for social interaction and relaxation that any child can get from riding. It can also provide a competitive edge, helping kids who may have been sheltered and not had the chance to build skills, play T-ball or soccer, or get involved in team sports. And as a means for providing therapy—from developing muscular strength, to movement patterns, to balance and rhythm—as well as achieving educational goals, the value of horseback riding is, in some ways, unsurpassed.

From the moment a child puts on a riding helmet and is helped into the saddle, each riding session is individually tailored to work toward objectives and goals deemed appropriate for the child. The basis is the assessment process, which combines input from the parents, members of the therapeutic riding team— including a certified riding instructor, therapists on staff or available as consultants, and volunteers who assist with each lesson—and the child herself.

Far greater than what people might imagine, therapeutic riding's range of specific benefits to a child with special needs can be considerable. Whereas for youngsters in general, lessons at a typical boarding stable are focused on developing independent riding skills, with therapeutic riding the potential is much broader. Physically, the horse's movement has a dynamic effect on the rider's body: the horse's gait naturally moves the rider's pelvis forward and back and side to side and rotates it in a way that cannot be duplicated by any other therapeutic means. When applied specifically as a component activity of therapeutic riding, it is called hippotherapy and is conducted in the presence of a professional therapist.

In its purest sense, in hippotherapy the rider is passive, with the therapist directing the movement of the horse to create change in the rider's body. However, depending on the individual situation, some therapists add to the hippotherapy model, asking the client to perform certain tasks while on horseback.

As any rider will tell you, a horse's movements affect the senses, something that can be used in therapeutic riding to help a child cope with a variety of sensory integration issues. For instance, a horse with a smooth gait and consistent pace may be able to help a child establish rhythm. Conversely, one with a rough gait may be useful in assisting the rider to organize and integrate sensory input. In addition, exploring movement while on the horse can aid in improving body awareness.

For any child, riding can provide a measure of self-confidence unlike any other activity, and for those with special needs, the emotional payoff can be even greater. Professionals attribute this to the risk factor and the inherent challenge riding presents. Though in therapeutic riding those risks are minimized, even there they can never be eliminated. Accepting the risks helps a rider overcome fear and anxiety, and it promotes a better self-image. Bonding with the horse, plus the relationships that develop with staff and volunteers at these riding centers, adds to a positive experience.

Again, in an extension of a horse's ability to inspire any child to learn, in a therapeutic setting, nonriding educational goals can be incorporated into both mounted and unmounted activities. Such things as letter recognition and sequencing, problem solving, and using judgment and reason are just some of the skills that can be presented and practiced using riding-related situations.

Is Therapeutic Riding for Your Child?

Therapeutic riding can, without a doubt, help many children, perhaps for many years. But is it right for your child? It might be, but then again, it may be an activity that would not be suitable for your child, and that is something that has to be decided.

The first step is to talk with your child's physician and/or other health care providers to be sure that physically, cognitively, and behaviorally, horseback riding will be an appropriate activity. They can assess whether riding will be a potentially beneficial or harmful undertaking for your child or whether it is something you can explore further. In a very general sense, a child must have sufficient trunk support and head stability to sit on a dynamic, moving surface such as a horse's back. In some instances, tandem or back riding may be possible, where another individual sits behind the child, but even here a certain level of physical strength is required.

Some situations are untenable from the beginning, others will turn negative, still others can be saved by turning to an alternate activity. Every step of the way, from the time your child enters a program, trained staff will be watching her behavior, ready to make adjustments when indicated. For instance, a youngster with autism who doesn't have expressive language may find the sensory input too great yet not be able to say she doesn't want to get on the horse. Gauging the situation, it may be apparent that an alternate and graduated method may achieve the same goal. In this case, a child is saying "no" to riding, but horse-related activities may still be a benefit. By contrast, a child with extreme separation anxiety may simply not be able to continue in a program.

For a child to participate in a therapeutic riding program, she must have a level of compliance such that she does not create potentially hazardous situations, either for herself, the instructor and volunteer assistants or the horse. Uncontrolled seizures are another issue that would make riding a problem. Again, because a horse is a rather high, dynamic moving surface, the concern would be in getting the child off in time if a seizure occurred. Even more than the go-ahead from your child's medical team, which should be sought first, a trained riding staff will have the depth of experience to know when and what therapeutic riding activities can be beneficial and when they are not a viable option. Nobody wants your child hurt.

Choosing a Facility

Finding a therapeutic riding center for your youngster or a stable where such a program is offered is a lot like choosing any other stable (see chapter 2). You want a facility that is well maintained and well run, horses that are well cared for and proper for the job asked of them, and you want instructors who are competent and well trained.

However, as the parent of a child with special needs, finding a suitable stable will likely ask more of you than that. Indeed, there may be an excellent facility close at hand, but the reality is that there are far fewer therapeutic riding centers to choose from than there are stables with regular riding programs. In addition, there are safety features that must be in place, plus a number of other considerations.

GATHERING INFORMATION

With a green light from your child's physician and others on her own support team, how do you start moving forward with the idea of therapeutic riding? For starters, educate yourself as thoroughly as you can. NARHA can direct you to therapeutic riding programs in your area, either at independent centers or ones conducted at local riding stables. Or, if you find one on your own, you can contact NARHA (even if you are not a member), and it will tell you whether the instructor and facility are accredited and in good standing. Check out NARHA's Web site, www.narha.org, or call 800-369-RIDE. NARHA's official publication, *Strides*, which is a benefit of NARHA membership, can provide some excellent reading as well. *Strides* is also available without a NARHA membership for $34 per year (four issues), from NARHA, Inc., P.O. Box 33150, Denver, Colorado 80233.

Visit riding locations, talk with parents and staff, and read as much as you can. NARHA has accredited more than 670 programs across the country, a process that involves sending representatives to the site to review standards of safety and make sure they are in compliance. If your child is going to get involved in therapeutic riding, it makes good sense that it is at an accredited facility.

EVALUATING FACILITIES YOURSELF

Do your own evaluation of potential stables as well. Check the staff's credentials. Therapeutic riding instructors should be certified, and NARHA is the lead organization in this field. There should also be support staff: If your child has a physical disability, a facility with a physical therapist on staff or on call may be warranted. If your child's disability is behavioral, an occupational therapist may be helpful. Or if your child's problems are emotional, psychological, or mental health issues, a facility with a licensed mental health professional on board may be the proper choice.

You should set up an interview with the center's staff, and, if you can, watch a lesson or two. When you decide on the program that you want your child to join, you should expect a pre-lesson assessment, at which time you and the staff discuss expectations and goals—yours and your child's—and a plan for achieving them.

These centers often have waiting lists, so you will want to make your decision and put your child's name on a list as soon as is comfortable for you. While no one wants to see a child wait for something as potentially beneficial as therapeutic riding, it does speak to a positive situation: Overwhelmingly, the number of children with special needs who participate in such programs benefit from them, and the demand for them is growing.

Even if a facility is accredited, do take the time to double-check the physical surroundings yourself from a safety standpoint, particularly if the program is conducted on the premises of an area boarding stable and not in a facility used only for therapeutic riding. Is there a ramp for children who use wheelchairs or walkers? Is there an accessible bathroom? What equipment is available to transfer a rider from a wheelchair to a horse's back? An independent facility will have a platform that can be raised or lowered, or an overhead lift, but if this is a shared facility, does it have such a device?

You also need to find out if there is a weight limit for riders, as too much weight is potentially injurious to the horse. Such considerations are important because these highly trained animals need special care. Horses who can be used in the field of therapeutic riding must be tolerant, willing, and receptive to people of all sorts, far above the level of those in a regular riding program. Those who work with these horses will tell you they are one-in-a-million, and you will want to see them treated as such.

WHAT THERAPEUTIC RIDING COSTS

Expect to pay, per session, about the same as for a regular riding lesson. Many centers have scholarship programs and other ways to defray expenses for those who need assistance.

As for equipment, the only specific requirements are an ASTM/SEI-certified riding helmet and short leather boots or sturdy leather shoes with a heel. Centers frequently get donations of riding gear and undoubtedly can lend you a hat, and maybe even suitable riding boots. Check, of course, to make sure; or, if you prefer, you can buy your youngster what she'll need. If buying is your choice, you can find a schooling helmet and paddock boots at a local tack shop or from one of the suppliers listed in chapters 4 and 5. Other than that, make sure your child is dressed in comfortable pants and a shirt, plus a jacket, if the temperature dictates.

STABLES THAT DON'T MEASURE UP

No doubt, you have come to appreciate that operating a well-run therapeutic riding center is a very expensive undertaking. Unfortunately, there are unscrupulous people in this field, just like in other walks of life, willing to cut corners and jeopardize the well-being of those who are relying on them. Don't let it happen to your child!

As you look around a facility, keep an eye out for telltale signs that indicate you should find another center for your child. First, check for general cleanliness, just as you would in any other stable. If the facility is dirty and unkempt, look elsewhere. Next, monitor your impression of the instructor. Is he unprofessional looking? Are you suspicious that he may be using alcohol or other drugs? If yes to either of these questions, look elsewhere. And what about the horses? If they look unclean or unhealthy or if they are behaving in any way other than calm, quiet, bright-eyed, and happy, again, look elsewhere. And don't second-guess yourself or debate your reactions. Your child's welfare is too important for that.

If the facility doesn't request medical information on your child, if it doesn't require you to sign a release, if it doesn't do an intake evaluation, and if it doesn't ask for your input, you should be wary: These are also signs of a program with which you don't want to get involved.

Finally, if the instructor does not have credentials—in all likelihood, certification from NARHA—consider another facility. And to repeat, if you have any questions at all, NARHA is there to help you. While it is a membership organization, you do not have to be a member to get assistance.

Beginning a Program

A thorough intake process is a crucial step in designing a successful riding program for your child. To begin with, you and the staff need to review all pertinent documents, including your child's up-to-date medical history, as well as documents concerning liability insurance and any other information regarding the center. As appropriate to your child's condition, the staff should meet and talk with her and observe her in unmounted and mounted situations. In addition, you and the staff should discuss potential goals for your child, a process that will be revisited and adjusted, as needed, throughout her time at the center.

The actual conduct of a therapeutic riding session will vary from center to center. One place there will be mostly group sessions, at another a mix of group and private sessions. Some places run sessions combining children with and without special needs, again proving the equalizing force of the horse as all learn to ride. For those who need the help, volunteers function as an extension of the instructor; one leads the horse, and two act as sidewalkers, one at each side, holding the child in the saddle. For children who do not need special assistance, expect a session to include, once each child is mounted up, some exercises or other type of warm-up and a review of the previous session.

Most centers encourage consistent participation on the part of your child, probably amounting to one session a week. As with any riding situation, there is a sought-after continuum that's achieved when lessons are repeated at regular, frequent intervals. Professionals in therapeutic riding find that a lesson a week is a workable arrangement. Whether a center would think it useful for a child to ride less often would be something you would need to ask and for the center to decide. Many centers have financial aid programs, and this may be a factor in your decision to take your child to a particular facility.

Parents as a Part of the Therapeutic Riding Team

Because of your child's special needs, you are so much a part of her everyday life and you'd like to help her in this new endeavor. What can you do? Therapeutic riding centers encourage parents to stay connected to the program, communicating their thoughts to the staff and being open to what staff members have to say.

After the intake process, you should continue to share information that could help the riding instructor. This could include

Just Some Kids Riding Together

Integrated riding programs, where kids with and without disabilities ride together in a group, are useful in minimizing or erasing the differences, at least for a time, with everyone focusing on the same thing: learning how to ride. It's a center-by-center undertaking, and those that offer such programs usually publicize them through a local school or other appropriate organization.

Centers also welcome volunteers, sometimes even teenagers. Individual centers have different needs, as well as guidelines for who they want to help. But if you and your child are looking to do something rewarding, why not give them a call? Overall, centers try to pair volunteers with their interests and abilities, using them to help care for the horses or in the riding program.

current medical concerns of your child or any changes during the previous week that could affect the lesson. You should also participate in goal setting and revision, especially because goals for your child may well include some that can be addressed in a riding environment. It's important that you listen to feedback from the staff, including how sessions go and what improvements or detractions have become apparent. Granted, it will be frustrating at times, but try to be patient and not expect too much. Though dramatic changes do occur, more often improvements are small and incremental, occurring over a long period. If, of a given day, the instructor's review after a session isn't as good as you'd hoped, take it in the manner it's given, as part of an ongoing effort to help your child and give her as positive an experience as possible.

As to your role during a riding session, again it will vary with the center. At some places you will be asked to stay on the sidelines and watch, while other places may encourage your active participation. It depends on what, in their experience, works best. Therapeutic riding is a complex undertaking on the part of the instructor and support staff, and in any one session they will likely be addressing issues as varied as body strength and coordination, instruction, problem solving, self-esteem, and much more. From your distance, however, you may miss the fine-tuning. All you see, perhaps, is your child walking or trotting, round and round, week after week. "What's going on?" you wonder. "When will she canter?"

No matter how much you want to see it, she may not be ready, as an example, to canter. Realistically, it may simply not yet be within her capacity to achieve. The challenge is to determine, and sometimes later to reevaluate and reset, goals that are attainable. In that, the members of the therapeutic riding staff are the final arbiters. If you have chosen well, listen to them. They have your child's best interests at heart, and they will do their utmost to help her move forward.

After many lessons, you might look back and realize just how much your child has benefited from therapeutic riding. Whether it has been physically beneficial, whether it has improved her self-esteem and helped her to gain confidence in herself, or whether it has helped her in some other emotional way, hopefully, you will see that therapeutic riding is doing good things for your child.

Glossary of Horse and Riding Terms

aged   To be over ten years old, for a horse.

aids   Devices that are employed to influence the movement of a horse. Natural aids are the hands, legs, torso, and voice; artificial aids are crops, spurs, and martingales.

American Saddlebred   A flashy, high-stepping, three-gaited (walk, trot, and canter) or five-gaited (walk, trot, slow gait, rack, and canter) horse, now bred primarily for the show ring, in which it competes only on the flat. These horses were originally ridden in the United States by Southern plantation owners while inspecting their crops.

antisweat sheet   A covering made of extremely loose-woven cloth or coarse mesh that is draped over a wet or sweaty horse to help speed drying, while protecting the horse from getting chilled.

Appaloosa   A popular breed of pleasure horse noted for a spotted coat, of which there are six pattern types. Appaloosas were first bred by the Nez Perce Indians of the Palouse Valley in the American Northwest.

appendix   A horse produced from the mating of two recognized breeds, such as a Thoroughbred–Quarter Horse mix.

Arabian   A breed of relatively small horse with a muscular, compact body and a lively yet gentle disposition often called an Arab, that was originally bred in ancient Arabia.

bank   A natural obstacle, literally a mound of earth, found on cross-country courses. A bank usually has a gentle slope on the entry side, a plateau, and a steep descent on the exiting side.

barn sour   Being reluctant to leave the immediate vicinity of the barn. A horse that is barn sour may go a short distance, spin and run back to the barn, and even attempt to go right into his stall, despite the rider's efforts to stop him. This is particularly dangerous if the horse is ridden by children or inexperienced adults, who would have little chance of controlling him.

barrel racing   A rodeo event for women in which a mounted rider races through a series of sharp turns around three barrels in a cloverleaf pattern.

bascule   The arc of a horse's body over a jump. For it to be evident, the obstacle needs to be of a height sufficient so that the horse must round or "use" himself to clear it.

bat   A type of crop. Also known as a jumping bat or jockey's bat, it is shorter (about 15 inches in length) and stiffer than a riding crop, and has a wide, flexible leather tip.

bay   A horse of brownish color, ranging from light to dark, coupled with a black mane, tail, and lower legs, known as black points.

bedding   The material used on the floor of a stall, most commonly straw or wood shavings.

billets   The straps that buckle to the girth under the flap on each side of an English saddle.

bit   The mouthpiece of the bridle—usually made of metal or of rubber- or plastic-covered metal—to which both the cheekpieces of the bridle headstall and the reins are attached. Two common bits are the snaffle, requiring a single rein, and the pelham, which uses double reins.

blacksmith   One who shoes horses. Also called a farrier.

blanket   A heavy, contoured covering worn by a horse during cold weather, when not being ridden. Most blankets have interlinings of foam or fiberfill.

blue ribbon   An award given for first place in the United States.

boarder   A person who owns a horse kept at a stable.

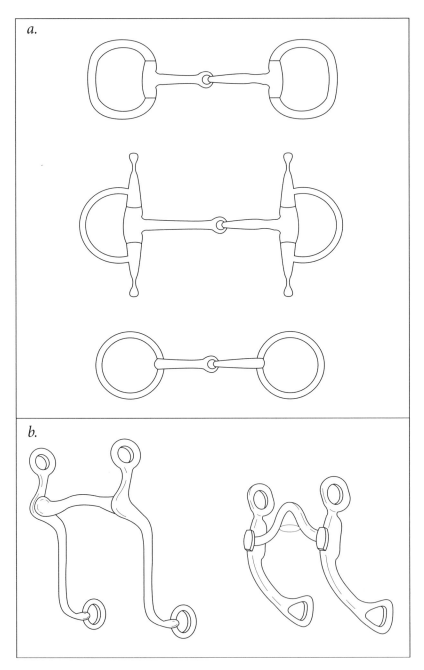

(a) English bits. (b) Western bits.

boots (1) Leg and hoof coverings a horse wears for protection, including shipping boots that cover the pastern and lower leg during transport; bell boots to cover the hooves; splint boots, for the inner lower leg; galloping boots, for the back of the lower front legs; and ankle boots. (2) Fitted coverings (usually of leather or rubber) for a rider's foot and lower leg. For English riding, knee-high black leather boots, either dress style with a plain toe and vamp, or field style with a short row of laces at the instep are proper. The same black leather boots can have mahogany-colored cuffs for hunting. Ankle-high, lace-up paddock boots are usually worn with chaps. Western boots have a higher heel and pointed toe and are made of fancy, tooled leather in a variety of colors.

bosal A type of Western noseband made of braided rawhide. The ends of the bosal are joined together by a rawhide knot that weighs the device. With reins attached, it is the simplest bitless bridle.

bouncer Two fences set close enough together so that a horse must jump in and out without taking a full stride in between.

breakaway stirrups Metal toe rests that hang at the ends of leather straps from each side of a saddle. They function like any English stirrup, except the outside bar opens against force. Children should use breakaway stirrups. That way, if they fall off their horse, their feet will be sprung free and will not get hung up in the stirrup. See *irons.*

breastplate A series of straps that keeps a saddle from sliding backward. A three-part leather strap encircles the horse's neck, from which additional straps buckle to either side of the saddle, and another runs between the horse's forelegs and attaches to the girth.

breeches Formfitting riding pants made of stretch fabric. Pronounced "britches."

bridle The headgear with which a horse is governed and which includes a bit and reins. The parts of an English bridle are the browband, noseband, headpiece or headstall, throat latch, cheek pieces, and reins. A Western bridle can have a browband or, if it doesn't, the headstall will have a split or fitted earpiece. If a

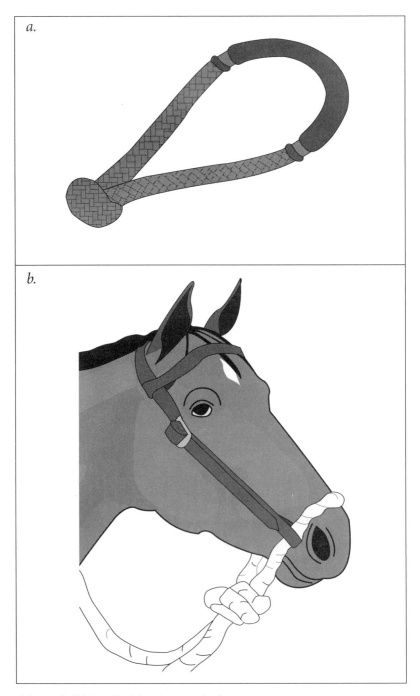

(a) Bosal. (b) Bosal with reins attached.

184

Western bridle has a bit, usually there is no noseband; the bridle can also be bitless. See *hackamore* and *bosal.*

broken line   In jumping, a curved path between two obstacles that are set at angles, rather than parallel to one another.

brush box   A long and narrow window box–like obstacle with shrubbery coming out the top. As a fence, it is usually combined with a straight rail above it.

buckskin   A breed of horse that is a light brown color, with a black stripe down the back, plus a dark mane, tail, and, usually, legs. There may be zebralike stripes behind the knees.

bute   Short for Butazolidin, the trade name for phenylbutazone, a common anti-inflammatory pain reliever. It is available by prescription in tablets or paste.

caliente   A hard hat with leather ear covers and chin strap, popular with jockeys and event riders. Brightly colored nylon covers are replaceable.

cannon bone   The long, vertical bone in each of the horse's lower legs, between the knee and the fetlock joint.

canter   A fast, three-beat gait, and one of the horse's natural gaits.

cantle   The raised portion of the saddle, behind the rider's seat.

cavaletti   Wooden poles laid on the ground at walk or trot strides apart and used in various training exercises. Also called trotting poles, they can be flat on the ground or slightly elevated. See also *ground poles.*

change reins   A command for riders to change direction in a ring, from clockwise to counterclockwise or vice versa.

chaps   Leather leggings that fasten across the hips, front and back. English, schooling, and polo chaps are fitted to the leg, with a full-length zipper from hip joint to ankle. Western chaps are wider at the foot and are often lavishly adorned with fringe and metal studs.

cheekpieces   Part of a bridle headstall, the ends of which buckle to the bit rings.

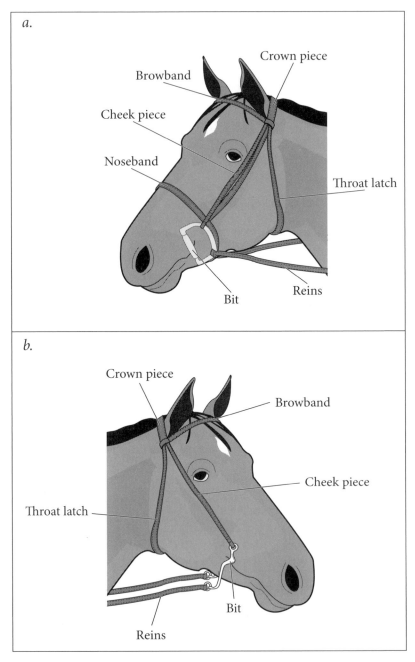

(a) English bridle. (b) Western bridle.

chestnut (1) A horse coloring that is reddish, ranging from light to dark, and bright to dull, with mane and tail of the same color. Can be referred to as a golden chestnut or liver chestnut. In Western riding it is called sorrel. (2) A rough, elongated, callous-like patch on the inside of each of a horse's legs, near the knee or hock. Like human fingerprints, each is unique. Thoroughbred racetracks use them as a form of identification.

chicken coop See *coop*.

chip A short, scrambling, out-of-rhythm last step before a fence. It is considered poor jumping form and causes a competitor to lose standing in a hunter or equitation class.

cinch See *girth*.

class At a horse show, an individual competition that a rider enters. A rider usually enters several classes at one show.

clipping Shaving a horse's body hair to eliminate the difficulty of getting a sweaty, damp horse dry in cold weather, along with the potential for a horse taking a chill. Various styles of clipping include a full-body clip, in which all the hair is shaved off, and a hunter clip, in which only the underbelly is shaved, and the hair on the top and sides of the neck, back, and rump are left for warmth.

clucking, chirping Sounds made by a rider to encourage a horse to move forward. These sounds should not be used in the company of others, when the cues might be taken by the wrong horse; they are forbidden in the show ring.

Clydesdale A heavy horse, originally bred in Scotland and used for draft and driving. In the United States, teams of Clydesdales have become popular for pulling the Budweiser beer wagon. They are also shown in driving competitions.

cob A small, stocky, short-legged type of horse. A cob should be of solid, sturdy build, with good bones.

cold-backed A horse with a back that is extremely sensitive to a rider's weight. When a rider sits in the saddle too quickly and heavily, such a horse may buckle.

cold blood   A horse other than a Thoroughbred or an Arabian, or a horse who does not have Arab, Turkoman, Anglo-Norman, or Spanish blood in his ancestry. Most of the draft breeds are cold-blooded. Ponies are not designated as either a warm or cold blood.

colic   Any abdominal distress. The common causes of colic generally include flatulence, a mass of hard food blocking the intestine, or a twisted intestine.

collected   Riding a horse with a steady contact on the reins, the neck flexed and the hocks well under his body, so that he is balanced and moving forward off his hind end.

colt   A male horse under four years old who has not been castrated.

combination fences   Three or more fences set up in a line, as a training device for horse and/or rider. Also called a gymnastic.

combined training   See *eventing.*

concussion   Stress on a horse's legs and feet due to repeated impact with the ground, particularly when the surface is hard or the horse has been jumping too much.

conformation   How a horse is proportioned. What is sought is a symmetrical, balanced combination of the parts of his body.

contact   Maintenance of tension on the reins, usually light, from the horse's mouth to the rider's hands, which gives the rider a feel of the mouth.

cooler   A wool throw that protects a horse from taking a chill when he is hot from a workout and the air is cool. A cooler can be contour fitted with a front buckle or straight cut, like a blanket, with tape ties.

coop   A fence with solid sides inclined toward a single ridge line, in an A-frame shape. It is jumped from the side, across the ridgeline. Also called a chicken coop.

cow-hocked   Viewed from the horse's rear, having hocks that are close together, so that the lower legs veer apart and the toes turn out.

cowhorse   A Western stock horse with agility, balance, and stamina to do ranch work, including cutting and calf roping. Quarter Horses prevail as cowhorses, along with Paints.

cribbing   The act of a horse biting or setting his teeth around an object and sucking air into his gut. Cribbing is considered a stable vice.

crop   A slim, relatively short (about 18 inches long) whip with a leather "feather" or fringe at the tip. Crops are used by English riders.

crossrail   Two jumping poles set on opposing diagonals between two standards to form an X. A crossrail is considered the simplest jump.

crosstie   A barn restraint that employs a length of webbing attached at one end to a wall or pillar. The free end has a snap that can be clipped to a horse's halter. Used in pairs, on either side of the head, crossties gently keep a horse in place while he is being groomed, shod, tacked up, or for other short-term needs. Crossties are also used to secure horses during trailering.

cups   Curved metal pieces in which jumping poles rest. The cups are welded to cuffs that are, in turn, attached to the standards with long metal pins.

curb chain   A short length of link chain, attached to a curb bit, and resting flat in the horse's chin groove. A curb chain is used with a full or Pelham bridle.

currycomb   A circular brush with metal teeth that is used to clean other brushes that groom a horse. A rubber curry is used directly on the horse's coat to bring dirt to the surface.

dam   The female parent of a foal. In describing a horse's breeding, you say that a horse is *by* (sire's name) *out of* (dam's name).

dandy brush   A hard-bristled brush that is used to remove the heaviest grime and hair.

dapple   On the horse's coat, splotches of a darker shade within the same color family, as in a dapple gray.

diagonal At the trot, the horse's shoulder being thrust forward at the same time that the rider is at the top of the post. When doing a posting trot on a curved line, the rider is on the correct diagonal if she has risen out of the saddle when the horse's outside shoulder is forward.

division At a horse show, a grouping of three or four related classes. Besides ribbons for each class, championship and reserve championship (first and second place) are awarded for a division, based on total points won from separate classes.

double bridle See *Weymouth bridle*.

draw reins A second set of reins attached to the girth as a training device to help a horse flex his neck and bring his head down. They are attached to the girth at each side of the horse below the saddle, then brought through the bit rings, and held by the rider along with the bridle reins.

dressage A classical discipline that develops a horse's balance and suppleness and that requires a harmonious partnership with his rider. Dressage is popular in and of itself, with horse shows devoted solely to dressage competition. Its study is also excellent preparation for jumping, hunting, and pleasure riding.

dressage arena An area used for dressage practice or competition. The large size is 60 meters by 20 meters, and the small size is 36 meters by 20 meters. Both are laid out with letters of the alphabet that guide the rider in the execution of various maneuvers.

driving Having horses in harness, for pleasure and competition, singly pulling carts, and in pairs and teams of four to eight pulling carriages. Draft horses, pony breeds, and Morgans are popular driving horses.

drop his head On approach to a jump, to lose contact with the horse's mouth.

dun A horse of light brown color, much like a Buckskin, but without the dark stripe down the back.

endurance riding   A competitive part of riding that tests the stamina and speed of a horse over long distances, sometimes as much as 50 to 100 miles. The horse must complete the distance in a specified time, monitored by vet checks along the way, and returning fit and healthy.

English hunt seat   The formal title for the style of riding used by hunters, jumpers, and equitation riders. A type of saddle, bridle, and other tack are particular to the style.

entry   A rider-and-horse pair entering a class at a show.

equine   (1) Of or pertaining to a horse. (2) A horse himself.

equitation   A style of riding for competition that is judged on the manner and performance of the rider over that of the horse. Also called hunter-seat, stock-seat, or saddle-seat equitation.

eventing   The triathlon of equestrian sport, a type of competition that tests the horse's and rider's ability at dressage, cross-country over obstacles, and stadium jumping. Also known as combined training.

extension   A strong, forward-reaching component of movement that is powered from the horse's hind quarters.

farrier   See *blacksmith*.

far side   See *off side*.

feed   Various grains plus hay that a horse eats.

FEI (Federation Equestre Internationale)   The world organization governing equestrian sport.

fetlock   The back of a horse's ankle joint. It is covered with hair that grows away from the body and, if not trimmed, forms a tuft.

filly   A female horse under four years of age.

flank   The side of a horse, where the belly joins the thigh.

flat work   Riding at the walk, trot, and canter without jumping any fences.

flexion   The act of rounding a horse's neck down and flexing his body left or right to enable him to carry himself in a supple, balanced manner.

floating teeth   Filing a horse's teeth to remove jagged spots that could hurt the inside of his mouth and make chewing difficult. This is done at the stable by an equine dentist or a veterinarian.

foal   A newborn horse up to one year old.

forehand   The head, neck, and shoulders of a horse. A horse is said to be "on the forehand" when he is bearing too much weight on these parts rather than pushing himself along with the power of his hindquarters.

forging   A clinking sound that occurs when a horse with shoes is not moving out sufficiently with his front legs, and a hind foot comes up and strikes a front foot. The clinking is the metal shoes hitting one another.

frame   The way a horse carries himself when he moves. A horse is in a simple frame when his head is flexed down; he is listening to the rider and moving in an organized manner. In dressage, as horse and rider advance, a more collected frame is required.

frog   The triangular area that protrudes from the sole of a horse's foot. It is a semisoft spongy structure that absorbs concussion and helps to maintain proper circulation in the foot and lower leg.

full bridle   See *Weymouth bridle.*

furacin   Short for nitrofurazone, a common topical antibacterial ointment.

gait   A sequence of foot movements by which a horse moves forward. The natural gaits are walk, trot, canter, and gallop. American Saddlebreds are also trained to slow gait and rack, and Standardbreds are trained to pace.

gallop   A four-beat gait that is faster than a canter and one of the horse's natural gaits.

gaskin   The part of the hind leg above the hock area and below the thigh.

gelding   A castrated male horse.

girth   (1) The leather "belt" that circles around a horse's belly and holds a saddle onto the horse. In Western riding it is called a cinch. (2) The measurement of a horse around the widest part of its ribcage.

girthbound   An adverse reaction to a girth being tightened too quickly. Also known as girthy. With a horse who is prone to this, the girth must be tightened gently, a hole at a time, and the animal must be walked in between.

goose rumped   Having a high-pitched rump and a tail that is set too low.

grade horse   A mixed breed of undetermined parentage.

grain   A seed or fruit of a cereal plant. Grains that are fed to horses are oats, barley, and bran. Sweet feed is a mix of grains bound together with molasses.

green   A horse that has little or no training. "Green over fences" refers to a horse who is just learning how to jump.

groom   (1) A person who takes care of horses, grooming them and mucking out their stalls. (2) To clean and polish a horse's body.

ground pole   A single pole laid on the ground, either directly under a jump or slightly in front of it, as an aid to horse and rider in determining the takeoff point for the jump. Also used in multiples for other training purposes. See *cavaletti*.

gymkhana   An all-games show for horse and rider, both English and Western, including such events as an egg-in-spoon race, musical "stalls" (like musical chairs), relays, bobbing for apples, and so on.

gymnastic   See *combination fences*.

hack   (1) To ride for pleasure in a relaxed fashion, with the horse on a very light contact or a loose rein. (2) A type of class at a show, such as bridle path hack or a hunter hack.

hackamore   A Western bridle that does not use a bit. It consists of a headstall and a bosal, or a noseband, made of plaited rawhide that is shaped like the outside of a tennis racquet with a weighty knot at the chin end and thin reins that are attached to the knot. The rider controls the horse through the bosal, which exerts pressure on the nose when the rider raises her hands.

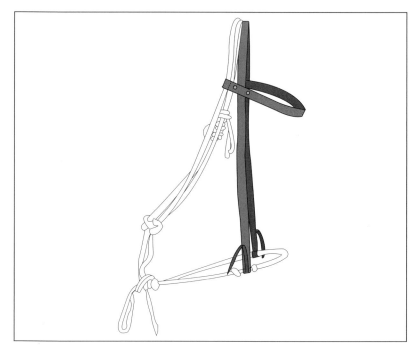

Hackamore bridle.

half chaps   Leg coverings made of heavy buckskin with Velcro, zipper, or buckle closures that cover the rider's lower leg from instep to just under the knee. They are a casual alternative to full chaps or high boots.

half school   The center of a ring. When a rider changes directions through that point, she frequently says, "Heads up, half school."

halter   A simplified bridle without bit or reins, usually worn by a horse in his stall or when turned out. It is made of leather, nylon webbing, a combination of the two, or rope.

hand   The measurement for horses and ponies, taken from level ground to the top of the withers. A hand equals 4 inches; fractions are given in inches. Thus, a horse who is 65 inches is 16 hands 1 inch, written 16.1 h.

hay   Dried grasses, put up in bales and fed to horses.

head shy   Being unable to be touched or even to tolerate quick movements about the head, without flinching and getting upset.

heaves   Reduced wind capacity due to ruptured air vesicles in the lungs. Heavey horses need to have the hay they eat wetted down to keep dust to a minimum. In addition, dust should be reduced in bedding.

hock   A joint in a horse's hind leg that looks like a reverse knee. It corresponds to the knee in the front leg.

hogsback   A spread fence that has low poles on either side of a single, higher center pole. As a cross-country fence, it is often solid, like a tiny barn with a raised roof.

hoof dressing   Commercial creams and liquids, applied topically, that moisturize the exterior of the hoof wall.

hoof pick   A metal hook, rather like a blunt can opener, that is used to clean dirt and debris from the sole of a horse's foot.

horn   A leather-covered steel protrusion at the front of a Western saddle, fastened to the pommel. It is intended to hold a coiled lasso. When the rider is holding a roped animal, the end of the lasso is tied to the horn.

horse   The general term for any equine.

hunt   The act of a group of riders and a pack of hounds traveling across open lands in search of a fox. Fox hunting, first popularized in Great Britain, has spread with little change to other parts of the world. In lieu of hunting an actual fox, today drag hunting after the scent is also done.

hunt cap   A velvet- or velveteen-covered, safety-approved hard hat, most commonly in black, with a peaked brim, and used for showing. For added protection, a child's hunt cap should have ear flaps and a chin strap.

hunter   Traditionally, a type of horse that is suitable for carrying a person to hounds. In the show ring, a hunter is a horse of good conformation, often a Thoroughbred or Thoroughbred cross, with an easy, rhythmic, consistent way of moving.

impulsion   Strong, controlled, forward movement of a horse, powered by the hindquarters.

in-and-out   Two fences set parallel to each other, with enough room between for the horse to jump over the first, take one full stride, and jump the second.

in deep   In riding two fences in a line, taking the first with a bigger-than-desirable jump. The landing puts the horse too far down the line, forcing him to lengthen or shorten the remaining strides so that the second jump will be even and the proper height for the fence.

indirect rein   A use of the reins that aids in bending a horse by angling the inside rein on a slightly diagonal path from the horse's mouth to the rider's inside hip. An indirect rein can be used in conjunction with an opposite opening rein.

in hand   Showing a horse in halter and lead and without his rider, to judge conformation and movement.

inside leg   The side of a rider or horse that is on the inside of a circle or track.

inside rein   The rider's rein on the inside of a circle or track.

irons   The metal toe rests that hang at the ends of leather straps from each side of a saddle. Also called stirrups. See also *breakaway stirrups*.

jog   The trot of a Western-trained horse. It has a shorter stride length and is less bouncy than that of its English counterpart, the trot, so the rider can sit to it comfortably.

jumper   A type of horse that is capable of clearing higher obstacles and negotiating tighter turns in more complicated courses than those for his hunter counterpart. Horses that compete as jumpers have to be athletic, powerful, fast, and agile.

keeper   A small, leather double loop. One end attaches to the cheekpiece of a bridle and the other slips over the wing of a full cheek snaffle, keeping the bit's wing in an upright position.

knockdown   A rail that is dislodged from the cups as a horse jumps a fence.

lead   The side of a horse on which the front leg stretches out farthest at the canter. Referred to as right lead and left lead.

lead line   (1)A handling and training device made of a long length of 1-inch nylon webbing, leather strapping, or heavy cotton rope, with or without a short length of metal chain at one end, and ending with a spring-action snap. A lead line is used when handling an untacked horse. Also used in rider training, it is attached to a horse's bridle at one end while the trainer holds the other end, thereby maintaining control of the horse while a rider is in the saddle. (2) A class at a horse show for very young children, who, attached to lead lines, are walked around on their ponies.

leg up   A boost of the left knee, held in a bent position, that helps a rider mount from the ground as she hoists her own weight upward.

leg wraps   Protection for a horse's lower leg that include polo wraps, used during workouts, and, if desired, at shows; and standing wraps over quilted padding, that are used like shipping boots, to protect from injury during transport or for overnight support.

line   The straight route across the center of a jump or between two fences separated by a set number of strides. See also *broken line*.

liner   A shaped covering used under a blanket for added warmth. It is made of fleece or some other soft material that will not chafe the horse.

liverpool   A water jump that consists of a shallow rectangular pond, frequently with a straight rail in front of it or across the middle.

lope   The canter of a Western-trained horse.

lungeing   Working a horse on a circle by attaching a long line to his bridle or halter. Lungeing can be a useful training tool to supple and balance a horse and also, when called for, to use up some exuberance.

lunge line   A long line of nylon or cotton webbing, of varying lengths between 20 and 30 feet, with the same chain and snap at one end (with or without a short length of chain) as a lead line. A lunge line is used when lungeing a horse.

mane   A horse's long hair, running the length of the neck.

mare   A female horse four years or over, whether or not she has had a foal.

martingale   A piece of tack that keeps a horse from tossing his head and evading the action of the bit. There are two types: standing martingale and running martingale.

Morgan   A small, sturdy breed of horse with exceptional stamina and a kind nature that makes an excellent all-around pleasure horse. Morgans are also popular with mounted police units.

mounting block   A platform, usually about 2 feet high, from which to mount a horse.

muck   To clean out wet bedding and manure from a stall.

muzzle   The nose, mouth, and chin area of a horse.

navicular   A bone within the front foot of a horse. If it becomes diseased, chronic lameness can result. Corrective shoeing can often alleviate navicular disease if it is diagnosed early.

near side   The left side of the horse.

neatsfoot oil   A leather conditioner, along with the similarly named neatsfoot oil compound. Both are useful, when warmed, to condition a new saddle or rejuvenate an older one, especially the undersides of the flaps and panels.

neck reining   Using pressure of the reins, held in one hand, against a horse's neck to cause him to move in the opposite direction. This type of reining is used in Western riding.

noseband   A part of a bridle that aids the action of the bit in the horse's mouth. Common types of nosebands for an English bridle include the cavesson, drop, flash, and figure eight. Western nosebands are the simple, cavesson style.

off course   At a show, the area outside the course, as shown in the posted diagram. When a horse and rider go off course in hunter-jumper competitions, they are disqualified. In dressage competitions, points are lost only within the portion of the test affected.

off side   The right side of a horse. Also called far side.

on the bit   Traveling in a balanced frame and moving forward off the hind end, with the head on the vertical. With this head carriage, a horse is accepting the bit. With the head other than on the vertical, the horse can be above the bit or behind the bit and either way can avoid the full effects of the bit.

on the buckle   Riding on a very loose rein, literally with hands near the buckle that joins the left and right reins.

on the flat   Riding without going over fences.

opening rein   A rein held away from the horse's body, usually in conjunction with an opposing indirect rein, to flex or bend a horse.

outside leg   The leg of a rider or horse that is on the outside of a circle or track.

outside rein   The rider's rein on the outside of the circle or track.

oxer   A spread fence made up of two horizontal poles, with the one nearer the horse on approach being lower than the farther pole. If the poles are the same height, it is a square oxer; if the poles are set on opposite diagonals, it is a Swedish oxer.

packer   An older horse, with years of training and experience, who knows the ropes and will "pack" a beginning rider around, so that the rider can learn without having to train the horse, as well.

paddling   As the horse trots forward, the circling motion of a front foot. Viewed head-on, the foot seems to fan inward slightly between footfalls.

paddock   A fenced-in outdoor area, where a horse can be left to graze or move about at leisure.

pads   (1) Pads that go on a horse's back, under the saddle, to absorb sweat and dirt and to provide some cushioning. They come in a wide variety of shapes and materials, ranging from thin quilted cotton rectangles to thick, shaped fleece pads and those with foam or gel cores, many of which change the way the saddle sits on the horse. (2) Protective pieces of plastic or leather that are secured between the hoof and the shoe. Usually, they fully cover the bottom of the front feet. Another version is rim pads, cut to fit under the shoe, for shock absorption or other reasons.

Paint   Also called a Pinto, a breed of horse that takes its name from the Spanish word for "painted." A Pinto is an all-purpose saddle horse of varying size and conformation, and its coloring is broken patches of white and black.

Palomino   A popular breed for Western riding. The horse has a golden body with white or flaxen mane and tail. Roy Rogers's horse Trigger was a famous Palomino.

parrot mouth   A condition in which a horse's upper incisor teeth extend over the lower ones. It is considered a physical abnormality that, in extreme cases, can affect chewing.

Paso Fino   A horse bred in Latin America for centuries and in the United States only since the late 1940s. The Paso Fino is a small, athletic horse with a high head carriage and a unique and natural, smooth, four-beat gait, known as the Paso Fino gait, which can be executed at three forward speeds.

pastern   The sloping part of a horse's foot, between the hoof and the fetlock joint.

pedigree   The breeding and performance of a horse, combined.

pellets A processed feed made up of various grains and other ingredients.

piebald A type of coat coloring found on a Pinto, specifically broken patches of black and white.

Pinto See *Paint.*

pleasure A type of class in competition that is judged against specific criteria describing a horse that is a pleasure to ride and that displays a pleasant attitude.

points (1) Units of scoring. Horses competing in numerous divisions at United States Equestrian Federation–recognized and other recognized shows can earn points toward yearend awards, both nationally and at the regional level. (2) Specific parts of a horse. The mane and tail are color points, the withers are a measuring point, and specific points along the horse's spine indicate soreness in extremities and other key areas of the body.

pole bending A rodeo event that requires horse and rider to weave in and out of six poles, set 21 feet apart, without knocking down a pole.

poll The highest point of a horse's head, between and just behind the ears.

polo pony A small, short-backed horse with the speed, agility, and courage necessary to play polo.

pommel The slightly raised front of the saddle, cut back around the horse's withers. In the Western saddle, the horn is attached to it.

pony A small horse, measuring 14.2 hands or less.

post To rise up and down with the movement of a horse at a trot.

post entry To sign up for a class at a show after the entries have closed. A late fee is charged for this.

poultice Liniment or other compound, wrapped with a large bandage, to draw the swelling or soreness from an inflamed part of a horse's body, usually a leg.

prepurchase exam   A thorough physical examination by a veterinarian of a horse being considered for purchase, at the request of the prospective buyer. Also called vetting or vetting out.

pull (mane)   To shorten and thin the mane (also the tail) by pulling out unwanted hairs by the roots with the aid of a small pulling comb.

quarter crack   A crack in the hoof wall, usually from the lower edge upward.

Quarter Horse   North America's most populous breed, which is compact and has massive, powerful hindquarters and strong shoulders. Popular for riding, ranch work, rodeos, and quarter-mile races, the Quarter Horse was developed by early colonists in Virginia and the Carolinas, who crossed mares of Spanish descent with imported English stallions.

quarter school   The midpoint between the half school and the outer edge of a riding ring.

quarter sheet   An abbreviated wool blanket, usually contoured, that tucks under the saddle and covers the back, rump, and flanks of a horse. Used when riding in cold weather, it is secured by the saddle's girth.

racehorse   A horse bred or kept for racing. Thoroughbreds race on the flat and in steeplechase races, Quarter Horses also race on the flat, at a quarter-mile, and Standardbreds race in harness as trotters and pacers.

ratcatcher   A detachable high collar worn with a riding shirt by hunter, jumper, and equitation riders.

red ribbon   (1) A ribbon that is tied in the tail of a horse who kicks when other horses come close. Used at shows, where the horse may be unknown to other riders. (2) The ribbon awarded for second place.

refusal   A horse's approach to a fence that culminates in him stopping or running out to the side to avoid jumping the fence.

registration   The listing of a horse with the official registry of that particular breed.

rein back   In Western riding, to cause the horse to back up on command, accomplished through the use of aids.

reining   The Western version of dressage and an Olympic-level competition. Reining horses execute intricate patterns that include circling, rollbacks, flying lead changes, spinning in place, and sliding stops.

reins   Straps fastened to a bit by which a rider or driver controls a horse. Reins are attached to either side of the bit and held by the rider. They can be laced, braided, or plain leather, and they can also be of cotton webbing or rubber-covered leather. With bits that require two sets of reins, each set is different; for example, one set is plain leather and the other set is laced so the rider can tell them apart quickly.

ringbone   A bony enlargement in the area of the pastern that can cause pain and lameness.

ring steward   A show ring assistant who relays the judge's commands to the competitors in a class.

roan   A color of a horse that is a mix of white and another color. In a blue roan, gray and white hairs mix to give an overall bluish effect. In a strawberry roan, a mix of chestnut and white hairs give a reddish effect.

roarer   A horse who makes a loud whistling or wheezing noise, especially during exercise. Roaring is due to a partial paralysis of the larynx muscles and is considered an unsoundness.

rodeo   A Western competition featuring bronco riding, calf roping, steer wrestling, Brahma bull riding, and barrel racing, among other events.

rolltop   A jump constructed to resemble the longitudinal quarter of a cylinder. The curved front side is frequently covered with fake turf or green shag carpet.

rub In jumping, to graze or touch a pole with a hoof, which may or may not result in the pole being knocked down.

rub rag A cloth used in grooming a horse.

rump The top, rounded area of a horse's hindquarters, from behind the point of hip to the base of the tail.

run out To approach a fence but, at the last moment, instead of jumping it, run out to one side or the other. Running out is a type of refusal.

saddle A girthed and usually padded and leather-covered seat for the rider of a horse. The parts of an English saddle are the pommel, seat, cantle, flaps, billets, knee rolls, and panels. The parts of a Western saddle are the horn, fork or swell, seat, cantle, skirts, fenders, and stirrups.

saddle soap Bar soap, available from tack shops, that is used specifically to clean leather and leaves little residue.

salt block A block of salt that is hung in a wall holder in a horse's stall. A large one can be set out in a pasture for several horses to lick. Licking a salt block, then drinking water, helps keep a horse from dehydrating.

schooling Practicing or training. At a show, there is usually a schooling ring, where competitors can practice before their classes.

schooling helmet A riding hat that has a safety-approved hard crown, a peaked visor, ear flaps, and a chin strap. The crown has an abrasion-resistant surface.

scope The power, thrust, and overall athleticism with which a horse clears a jump. A horse with scope, often called scopey, is one that embodies these traits.

serpentine A snaking exercise pattern that requires a horse to flex left and right and to bring his hindquarters under himself to execute tight turns.

shank Used for control, the metal chain at the end of some leads. See also *lead line*.

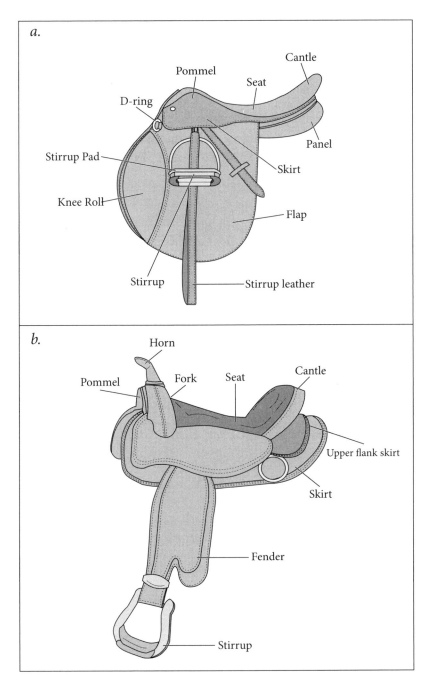

(a) English saddle. (b) Western saddle.

shavings   Pine shavings; used as bedding in a horse's stall.

sheet   A lightweight covering for a horse, secured with surcingles across the chest and under the belly, and made of cotton or cotton-blend duck cloth.

short coupled   Having a short back.

short stirrup   A classification at horse shows denoting riders twelve years and under.

shots   Vaccinations that should be given to a horse at least twice a year. The basic spring series usually includes eastern and western encephalomyelitis, tetanus, rabies, flu, and rhinopneuminitis. In the fall, flu and rhino shots are repeated. Depending on outbreaks of diseases in various parts of the country, other vaccinations may be added, such as ones for West Nile virus and Potomac Horse Fever.

show secretary   The person in charge at a horse show.

sickle hocked   A fault of conformation in which the hock protrudes and the lower hind leg is set on an angle to it. In a well-formed leg, the hock and lower leg are in line and perpendicular to the ground.

sidebone   Premature calcification of cartilage in the side-rear area of the pastern, usually of the front feet. It may not cause lameness but only remain as a blemish.

side reins   Adjustable reins that attach to the girth and the bit ring on either side of a horse. Used as a training aid, they help the horse to flex his head and neck.

sidesaddle   (1) A saddle that enables the rider to sit with both legs to one side rather than astride the horse. The saddle seat is wide and level from front to back, the rider's left foot rests in a stirrup, and the right left hooks around a large horn. (2) A riding discipline for women. Formal attire for riding sidesaddle includes a long skirt, fitted jacket, and low-crowned top hat.

sire   A horse's male parent.

skewbald   The coat coloring of a Pinto or Paint when the white is interspersed with any color other than black.

sorrel See *chestnut.*

spavin An inflammatory condition involving the hock joint. Bog spavin is a soft swelling, and bone spavin is a bony spur that affects the movement of the joint.

spread A fence built of parallel components, such as an oxer or a triple bar, that requires a horse to jump broadly.

spurs U-shaped metal devices that are worn by the rider above the heels of each boot. Spurs have protruding nobs at the back end that are used against the horse's sides to encourage him to move forward, preferably from the hindquarters. English spurs have small protrusions. Western spurs are overall larger and much fancier.

stable vices See *vices.*

stall Accommodations for a horse. A stall can be either a straight stall, which is fairly narrow, or a box stall, which is roomy enough for a horse to move around.

stallion A male horse who is not castrated and is four years or older.

Standardbred A breed of harness racing horses that traces its origin to the cross between the English Thoroughbred, the Messenger, and the Narragansett Pacer some two hundred years ago. The horse has a longish body, deep girth, powerful hindquarters, and fairly short, strong legs. Many of the breed both trot and pace.

standards The upright structures to either side of the rail, panel, or other horizontal part of a fence that a horse jumps. They can be single posts or more elaborate designs. The cups that hold the jumping poles are attached to the standards.

steeplechase A race of designated length in which horses gallop over solid brush hurdles.

steward See *ring steward.*

stifle A muscle joint in the area of the flank. When weak, it can be strengthened through extended periods of trotting.

stirrups   See *irons.*

stock tie   A white tie with wide tails that is tied around the neck ascot-style, the tails secured with a bar pin. It is worn in place of a ratcatcher for hunting and dressage.

stone bruise   A bruise to the underside of the foot. It can occur due to excessive jumping on hard ground or hitting a rock. Horses with soft soles are often shod with pads to reduce the risk of bruising.

stride   The amount of ground a horse covers in one step. At the canter, the average stride for a full-sized horse is 12 feet.

stud   A stallion who is breeding mares.

supplements   Vitamins and other additives given to a horse besides his regular diet of grain and hay.

surcingle   A wide nylon or elastic strap with a toggle-type fastener that holds blankets in place. A lungeing surcingle has a padded underside and rings for attaching side reins.

tack   All the equipment used on a horse when riding. This includes the saddle, girth, stirrups, and bridle, plus optional items, such as a martingale, side reins, or draw reins. Informally, tack has come to mean all equipment that is horse related, as in that carried in tack shops.

Thoroughbred   A breed evolved in England through the crossing of native mares with stallions from the Middle East. Thoroughbreds are famous for their use as racehorses, and they are some of the most beautiful horses in the world. Three are considered the foundation sires: the Byerley Turk, the Darley Arabian, and the Godolphin Arabian. With the exception of the Arabian, the Thoroughbred has influenced other breeds more than any other horse.

thrush   A disease that lodges in the crevices around the frog of the foot. If left untreated, it can cause lameness.

touch   See *rub.*

trailer   A conveyance for transporting horses that is hitched to the back of a car or small truck. The most common are two-horse trailers, gooseneck trailers, and stock trailers. The latter carries several horses in one large, open space in which each is secured to the trailer's side by a single crosstie clipped to the horse's halter.

transition   The changing of a horse's gait. Going from a walk to a trot, and a trot to a canter, are known as upward transitions. In reverse, from a canter to a trot, and a trot to a walk, are downward transitions.

trot   A two-beat gate, in speed between the walk and the canter, and one of a horse's natural gaits.

trotting poles   See *cavaletti* and *ground poles.*

turn out   To put a horse in an outdoor paddock or other enclosed area to graze and relax.

unsound   Having an abnormality serious enough to adversely affect the serviceability and salability of a horse.

upright   A type of jump that tests a horse's ability to jump high, as well as the accuracy of horse and rider in finding a takeoff spot, which is a more difficult challenge with uprights than with spread fences. Also called a vertical.

USEF (United States Equestrian Federation)   The national governing body for equestrian sport in the United States. Formerly the American Horse Shows Association, USEF governs twenty-seven disciplines and breeds.

van   Self-contained horse transport. Various-sized vans can carry six, eight, or twelve horses.

vaulting   A recreational and competitive discipline in which gymnastics and dance movements are performed on the back of a moving horse.

Venice turpentine   A compound the consistency of thick shellac that is painted on the underside of the hoof to help toughen it.

vertical   See *upright.*

vetting out See *prepurchase exam.*

vices Objectionable habits found in some horses in a stall. Though not considered serious enough to be called unsound-nesses, if left unattended they can affect a horse's health and well-being. Also called stable vices.

walk A four-beat gait, slowest of the horse's natural gaits.

wall-eyed Having eyes that are set very far apart.

warm blood Horses with Thoroughbred, Arabian, Anglo-Norman, Paso Fino, Turkoman, or Spanish stock in their lineage. Careful crossing of hot bloods (Thoroughbreds and Arabians) and cold bloods (draft horses, predominantly) has produced this grouping, which includes Hanovarians, Oldenburgs, Trakehners, and Swedish Warmbloods, along with a number of other breeds.

weanling A foal from the time he is weaned until he is one year old.

weaving The rhythmic movement from side to side of a horse in his stall. Weaving is considered a vice.

Western stock seat The formal name for all Western riding. A type of saddle, bridle, and other tack are particular to the style.

Weymouth bridle A bridle that consists of two bits, a bridoon and a curb, plus a curb chain. Separate reins attach to each bit. Also called a full bridle or double bridle.

whip A training aid, longer than a crop and tapering to a very slim end with feathers of string, that is used to drive a horse forward. Crops of varying lengths are used in dressage. There are also lungeing whips, 5 or 6 feet long, with rope tails of equal length, that are used to drive a horse forward on a lunge line.

wind The lung capacity and stamina of a horse.

wind puffs Soft, puffy swellings in the area of the fetlock joint, on either front or back legs. Considered a blemish, they can be the result of too much wear and tear on a horse.

winging   The outward circling of a front foot as a horse trots forward.

wishing well   A popular jump in which a horse jumps the "well" between the standards, that are camouflaged to look like castle turrets. It is similar to the wall, in that its solid appearance encourages a bold jumping effort.

withers   The V-shaped bones between the base of the neck and the back. A horse is measured from the ground to this point.

wormer   An oral medication in paste or liquid form that is used periodically to rid a horse of intestinal parasites. Owners frequently administer paste wormers themselves, while tube worming is done by a veterinarian.

yearling   A horse from his first to his second birthday. According to the Jockey Club, all registered Thoroughbreds are one year old on January 1, regardless of their actual date of birth in the previous year.

Index